SCOTTISH WRITERS

Editor
DAVID DAICHES

ALEXANDER MONTGOMERIE

R. D. S. JACK

SCOTTISH ACADEMIC PRESS

EDINBURGH

Published by
Scottish Academic Press Ltd
33 Montgomery Street, Edinburgh EH7 5JX

First Published 1985
SBN 7073 0367 2

Jack, R. D. S.
    Alexander Montgomerie.—(Scottish writers)
    1. Montgomerie, Alexander—Criticism and interpretation
        I. Title   II. Series
        821′.3   PR5029.M8

    ISBN 0–7073–0367–2

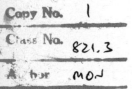
Printed in Great Britain by
Clark Constable, Edinburgh and London

CONTENTS

ACKNOWLEDGEMENT

The Scottish Academic Press acknowledges the financial assistance of the Scottish Arts Council in the publication of this volume.

As no likeness of Montgomerie has yet been discovered, the artist's impression on the cover is based on contemporary portraits.

PREFACE

In two important ways this book differs from those which have preceded and accompanied it in the series. Montgomerie is not established among the leading Scottish writers; nor is there a reliable modern edition of his works. The wider implications of this position are discussed in Chapter 6. Here I am concerned with the immediate, practical consequences as they have affected my approach and method of presentation.

As most of his work exists only in manuscript form and in Scottish Text Society (STS) editions, which are out of print and therefore not readily available, I have adopted a more descriptive approach than usual, not presuming that the reader will necessarily be acquainted with the poems concerned. The exception to this is *The Cherrie and the Slae* whose wider popularity has permitted me to assume some prior knowledge. Even here, however, a brief account of the poem accompanies the in-depth analysis. I have done this as I consider the book must have two functions—to make a contribution to the regrettably small canon of Montgomerie criticism but also to encourage the general reader and student to look at his verse for the first time.

The unsatisfactory textual situation has posed some problems. Cranstoun's edition of the Ker MS, which contains almost all of the poet's shorter verse, is not wholly reliable and so I have returned to the MS itself for all quotations. The references which follow these quotations do, however, for ease of reference, follow Cranstoun's divisions and numbering—MP = Miscellaneous Poems; DP = Devotional Poems; S = Sonnets. The MS has been cropped in such a way that the end of some lines is missing. Where this is the case and the reading is conjectural, the word or words concerned are enclosed in square brackets. For *The Flyting betwixt Montgomery and Polwart* I have adopted a composite text, using the first Hart edition of 1621 (H) for the opening section and the Tullibardine MS (T), which does not contain that section, for the rest. I have followed my own edition in *A Choice of Scottish Verse 1560–1660* for *The Cherrie and the Slae*. To aid understanding I have regularised spellings containing u, v and w or i and j; modernised punctuation; extended contractions and only followed the original capitalisation when it was clear that a particular stress was intended.

In writing the book I have incurred more debts than can be acknowledged. Parts of Chapter 3 have appeared earlier in a somewhat different form and I am grateful to the editors and publishers of *The Review of English Studies* and *The Scottish Literary Journal* for allowing me to reprint short extracts from the articles concerned. Many scholars aided me but I should like particularly to thank Jonquil Bevan, Murray Chalmers, Mark Dilworth, Gordon Donaldson, John Durkan, Alastair Fowler, J. T. D. Hall, Allan Hood, John MacQueen and Peter Sharratt. Jeanette Syme and Jill Strobridge typed the manuscript with much skill and care. Finally, as always, my wife gave me support and encouragement throughout.

R. D. S. J.

CHAPTER I

BIOGRAPHY

The most convenient way of introducing the life of
Alexander Montgomerie, the most talented Scottish poet
of the late sixteenth century, is to quote two extracts from
poems composed by James VI.

> Give patient care to sumething I man   must
>   saye,
> Beloved Sanders maistre of our art,
> The mouse did helpe the lion on a daye,
> So I protest ye take it in good part
> My admonition, cumming from a hart
> That wishes well to yow and all your
>   craft . . .
>
> (II, 120)
>
> What drowsie sleepe doth syle your eyes   cover up
>   allace
> Ye sacred brethren of Castalian band
> And shall the prince of poëts in our land
> Goe thus to grave unmurned in anie   unmourned
>   cace?
> No; whett your pens ye imps of
>   heavenlie grace
> And toone me up your sweete resound-
>   ing strings
> And mount him so on your immortall
>   wings
> That ever he may live in everie place.[1]
>
> (II, 107)

Montgomerie is the subject of both works. In each, the king
hails him as a leading practitioner within a group of poets.

But the tone and topic suggest changed circumstances. In the first, there is no hint of division. The king refers to him by a nickname, Sanders, and presumes that any criticism will be generously accepted. In the second, he discusses his death, lamenting the silence with which other members of the "Castalian band" have greeted it. The note he sounds is one of muted outrage and he accepts that Montgomerie is no longer automatically included in the group.

The first of these poems must have been written before 1584, as James uses a quotation from it in his critical treatise *The Reulis and Cautelis*, which was published in that year. It belongs, therefore, to the king's youth, a time when he built up his band of poets and established himself as their Maecenas or patron. Then, Montgomerie was regarded as his poetic tutor and this particular piece, which concerns the older writer's bragging about the speed of his brown horse, specifically addresses him as the "maister poete".

'What drowsie sleepe', on the other hand, is an epitaph, composed in 1598, the year of Montgomerie's death. By then political and religious tensions had driven him out of royal favour and away from the centre of the Castalian band. Despite these differences which forced James, as monarch, to expel his "beloved Sanders", he clearly states that, as poet, he still maintains the high opinion of his work, which first led them into friendship. Other Castalians now have his royal permission to make similar expressions of regret.

In broad terms, then, the story of Montgomerie's life would not look out of place in Boccaccio's *De Casibus Virorum Illustrium*. This chapter will trace the poet's fall from prominence, drawing attention to the various forces which caused it. But the fact that James had created an inner group of poets at the Scottish Court is at all times relevant to the study. It is the existence of this group with its friendly nicknames, its in-jokes and implicit hierarchies which made Montgomerie's later exile more difficult to bear. In particular, such expulsion did imply the loss of royal favour, as the poet himself complains:

> ȝit ȝe haif sene his Grace oft for me send,
> Quhen he took plesure into poesie.
> Quhill Tyme may serve, perforce I must
>   refrane,
> That pleis his Grace, I come to Court
>   agane.

(S XXVI)

This is to view the situation primarily in personal terms. The Castalian band had, as its major poetic aim, the task of making Scottish writing once more revered at home and abroad. In this context, James's *Reulis and Cautelis* were a critical statement emphasising Scotland's readiness to make its unique contribution to the Renaissance. James and his followers were aware of the great Scottish writers of the past—notably Henryson, Dunbar and Lindsay—but they were also anxious to look forward with Du Bartas, Ronsard, Gascoigne and Ascham. In their anxiety both to imitate foreign models and to produce original work reflecting the latest advances in poetry or prose Montgomerie, John Stewart of Baldynneis, William Fowler, William Alexander and the English brothers Robert and Thomas Hudson proved themselves part of this new literary adventure. When he was subsequently excluded from their number, Montgomerie experienced a sense of poetic isolation every bit as grievous as the loss of royal friendship or his place at court.

Little is definitely known about the poet's early life, so it is prudent to begin with certainties. We know that he was born in Hessilheid Castle, and in her Testament of 27 August 1583, Margaret Fraser, wife of John Montgomrie, 4th Laird of Hessilheid, appoints "Alexander Montgummerie hir lauchfull sone" as executor.[2] This means that on the maternal side, Montgomerie was directly descended from John Stewart of Derneley and so was distantly related

to King James. His father also was a noble, belonging to
the cadet branch of the powerful Ayrshire Eglinton family.
Alexander, however, was the third son in a family of five
and this junior position probably played its part in
determining that he should follow a martial career.

His date of birth cannot definitely be established. He
was born before Parish Records were regularly kept and
therefore no documentary proof is available. But two
pieces of evidence enable us to give a fairly exact
approximation. Two (and possibly three) of his poems
appear in the original part of the Bannatyne MS, which
was transcribed in 1568, and their presence in such a
prestigious collection has led most researchers to suggest a
birth date around 1545, thus supposing that the poems
were composed when the poet was in his early twenties.
This conclusion must now be weighed against the
discovery of five Latin poems written by Thomas Duff, a
Benedictine monk in the Scottish Abbey of St James at
Würzburg.[3] These were composed before 1614 and deal
with Montgomerie's life in some detail. In the fourth,
Duff refers to the poet's desire to become a monk in the
Würzburg community and asserts that he would have
done so "piam iuventam" (in his prime), had he not met
an untimely death. Montgomerie, as we shall see, died in
1598. If we adhere to the 1545 birth date, we must also
accept an age over 50 as the sixteenth-century definition
of "piam iuventam", while if we advance the date to the
early 1550s, we are faced with precocious contributions
to Bannatyne. I incline towards a later date, as poetic
reputations were often secured in comparative youth at
that period.

If Montgomerie's work was well enough known to be
included in the Bannatyne MS, then he must have been an
acknowledged poet in the reign of Mary. During the
troubled years between Mary's abdication and the seizing
of James by the Ruthven Raiders in 1582, we can plot
the poet's triple career as soldier, courtier and poet in

reasonable detail. In the first capacity he seems to have served in Argyll and the highlands, but also (if we can identify him with the narrator of one of his early dramatic poems) to have travelled widely in Europe. This last hypothesis is supported by Duff, who declares that he served for some years abroad, forsaking his original Calvinism to become a Catholic. This conversion was brought about by the teaching of learned Spain ("docta Hyspania"), where he found ready acceptance in the circles of King Philip ("in arce Philippi").

In assessing Duff's evidence, it is wise to heed Dilworth's warning that "the robust sectarian spirit of the author does not lend itself to objectivity",[4] but neither Montgomerie's military career (he is frequently referred to as captain), his wide travelling nor his conversion are seriously in doubt. Indeed, he may have been involved in a Catholic plot as early as 1580. At that date he was involved in a strange transaction with a Southampton merchant, Henry Gyllis. In partnership with two others, he bought from Gyllis a vessel called the *James Bonaventor*. Now, 1580 was the year in which the Jesuits were making a sustained effort to root out Protestantism in Scotland and England. Part of this plan involved restoring Mary, Queen of Scots to the throne and it has been argued that the poet's purchase may have been linked to these intrigues.[5] This is possible, but the only tangible evidence consists of two legal records, dated respectively November and December, 1584.[6] They deal only with financial matters and prove that if there were a plot Gyllis must have been ignorant of it, because he has openly consulted the English admiralty about the transaction. Equally, Montgomerie, who was at that date officially a "sirvitor to the Kings Maiestie", could scarcely have been suspected of having plotted James's replacement by a mother whom the king had been taught to hate. The poet's early complicity in Catholic plotting is, therefore, possible but by no means certain.

In fact, relations between James and Montgomerie were

at their most cordial in the late 70s and early 80s. Before 1583, it is true, he is never listed among the king's personal household but he was a respected courtier. In less fortunate days, he was wistfully to recall this eminence when bidding a poetic farewell to the Court circle:

> Shirs, ȝe haif sene me griter with his
>   Grace,
>
former
> And with ȝour umquhyle Maister, to,
>   and myne
> Quha thoght the Poet somtyme worth
>   his place,
>
since then
> Suppose ȝe sie they shot him out sensyne.
>
>   (S XVII)

The "umquhyle Maister" may be Esmé Stuart, Duke of Lennox, mentioned earlier in the sonnet and one whose influence over the king was considerable. The last line quoted would then refer to Lennox's expulsion by the Protestant Lords in the aftermath of the Ruthven Raid in 1582.[7] Certainly, major recognition as a writer came when Lennox and the king were enjoying their friendship to the full and the former was imbuing James with a love for the Pléiade and drawing him away from the Latin dominated teaching of George Buchanan. Montgomerie's own verse is influenced by French authors, most notably Marot and Ronsard, and some of his adaptations of their work (for example a sonnet which can definitely be assigned to 1582) belong to this period. James found in Montgomerie an established poet, who could share his newfound taste for vernacular verse and guide his hesitant steps as a 'prentise-poet'.

Nor did the "maister poete" hide his light under a bushel. Three public poems were composed at this time. Both 'The Navigatioun' and 'A Cartell of the thre ventrous knichts' were written as part of court entertainments designed to please a youthful king. Also, he engaged with

Sir Patrick Hume of Polwarth in a flyting, or open slanging match between two poets. These contests were designed not to convey real enmity but to exhibit poetic skills, and the court of James IV had earlier enjoyed a similar display involving William Dunbar and Walter Kennedy. Both the approximate date of the later contest and the king's enthusiasm for it can be gauged from the fact that he included an extract in his *Reulis and Cautelis* of 1584, as a model for 'Tumbling Verse'.[8]

The private side of Montgomerie's relationship with James is just as thoroughly documented. Mrs Shire has shown how he took on the rôle of Master and James that of apprentice; that they adopted nicknames—Montgomerie being Rob Stene and the king, William Mow—and that relations were so close that each felt free jokingly to chide the other. 'An admonition to the Master poët to be warr of great bragging' gives the best example of the relaxed atmosphere in which the poetic game was conducted. There James draws a witty picture of the boastful Montgomerie and makes the final defeat of his horse even more ridiculous by setting it within a framework of Virgilian epic. Yet the underlying note of respect remains. This is a joke against the acknowledged leader of the poetic band. Thus, the opening fable of the lion and the mouse, earlier cited, establishes Montgomerie's power rather than the king's. Elsewhere James appeals to the laws of friendship:

> A friend is aye best knowen in tyme of
>   neede
> Which is the cause that gars me take
>   such caire.

> (II, 122)

James was quite capable of curtly admonishing fellow writers whose work displeased him. For example, he wrote a blunt sonnet, warning Sir William Alexander that his work was metrically inadequate and too heavily angli-

cised.[9] But, although Montgomerie's character may sometimes be satirised, the tone always suggests "a hart that
wishes well" and James would no sooner have criticised
the verse of his 'maister' than he might have challenged
George Buchanan's skill in Latin.

In 1584, then, to use one of Montgomerie's favourite
metaphors, he found himself at the zenith of Fortune's
wheel. Acknowledged as soldier, courtier and poet, he
must have viewed with pride the publication in that year of
James's *Essayes of a Prentise*. He contributed one of the
introductory sonnets but, more important, he must have
known that in styling himself 'prentise', the king acknowledged his own mastery, along with that of Lennox. And if
the power of the latter's influence is directly expressed in
the *Phoenix*, an elegy which ranks as one of James's best
works, his own important rôle in moulding the royal talent
is evident in the critical essay, *The Reulis and Cautelis*.

The significance of this work for Scottish courtly writing
will be discussed later. In this context, it is only important,
that when James is seeking outstanding examples of the
poetic modes he wants to highlight, four of the seven
chosen stanzas come from the verse of his leading poet.
Montgomerie's work is used not only to illustrate
"Tumbling verse", but also "Troilus verse", verse suitable
for "Materis of Love" and for "brokin verse". James's
intention is to encapsulate the finest work available, so that
he may point the way forward for lesser members of the
Castalian band. The fact that Montgomerie dominates
this crucial section proves more forcefully than any words
of praise, that he is regarded as the finest poet of his day;
the one best fitted to lead the recently formed group into
the planned Renaissance.

And so, for a while, he did. A member of the royal
household since 1583, he had also been granted a pension
drawn from the revenues of the Bishopric of Glasgow. But
while the 'smithy' of the Castalian band was now working
at full heat,[10] changing religious pressures began to

impinge upon his career. As the power of the Protestant Lords grew, so James sought to maintain a policy of conciliation. In particular, as Gordon Donaldson notes, he "sought to maintain lines of communication, direct or indirect, with the Pope and with continental princes, and it was partly for this reason that in 1587 he had taken into his favour the exiled Archbishop of Glasgow . . . and the exiled Bishops of Ross and Dunblane".[11] Montgomerie was a courtier trusted by James and Philip alike. He was also a tried soldier with known Catholic sympathies. What better man to entrust with an undercover mission, aimed at placating the king of Spain, who was known to be concerned at the recent advances made by Protestantism in Scotland? This is almost certainly why the king granted to "Capitane Alexr. Montgomerie . . . his maiesties licence to depairt and pass of this realme to the pairtis of france, flanderis, spane and utheris beyond sey for the space of fyve 3eiris þaireftir".[12]

James's intentions seem reasonably clear. Montgomerie was, among other things, to reassure Philip of the king's desire to maintain cordial relations with Spain. Perhaps he was also to contact Betoun in France conveying the latest news about the Glasgow see. But all this could only progress satisfactorily if the true nature of the journey remained unknown in England, for the last thing the 'successor' to the English throne wanted was to reveal himself as a sympathiser with Elizabeth's arch enemy.

The worst happened. In June 1586 the boat carrying him was intercepted by an English vessel between Gravesend and the Brill. Lord Cecil reported that on it he found, along with "six score Scottish soldiers":

> one Montgomery, one as he saith himself, near in credit and place to the King of Scotland; one that hath served in the Low Countries and captain of that ship. There is great suspicion, as the Scottish man saith, that he was 'a taking man,' notwithstanding his

excuse was that being without a pilot, he durst not put
in, neither into Flushing nor the Brill . . .[13]

Contraband was found on board, suggesting that the poet
had decided to combine political duties with some private
enterprise; Montgomerie went off with his documents to
plead his case before the authorities, while Cecil remained
to guard the Scottish boat.

The poet's position was a dire one. If the papers he
carried referred explicitly to the purpose of his journey, he
was in even deeper trouble; if they did not, any 'character
references' would be little use in the face of a piracy charge.
Foreseeably he was put in jail. In his heart of hearts he
must have known that direct aid from the royal Castalian
was unlikely. For James to intervene would have involved
him in explaining aspects of his policy which had to remain
secret if a breach with England were to be avoided. But the
poet was still imprisoned by March 1589 and understand-
ably was then feeling bitter towards those whom he
counted his friends:

> Remembring me whair I haif bene
> Both lykit and belov't,
since then   And now sensyne what I haif sene,
roused to passion   My mynd may be commov't.
> If ony of my dolour dout,
> Let ilkane sey thair tym about:
> Perhaps whois stomok is most stout,
> Its Patience may be prov't.
>
>   (M.P.V)

This sense of betrayal was compounded when he learned
that a new Archbishop of Glasgow had been appointed
and that he had seized the poet's pension for 1586 and
1587. To Montgomerie this was further proof that his royal
patron had failed him. When he did return to Scotland and
finally lost all claims to that pension after lengthy
litigation, his fury at James's impotence found powerful
poetic expression:

The worst is ill, if this be bot the best.
Is this the frute, Sir, of your first affec-
tione,
My Pensioun perish under your protec-
tio[ne?].

(S XVI)

The emotion is perfectly understandable but the case was in fact much more complex than Montgomerie ever allowed and James's efforts on his behalf, though ultimately unsuccessful, not inconsiderable.[14]

To begin with, when he granted Montgomerie his pension in 1583. James was flying in the face of Common Law. No one could grant pensions from a see which was vacant, as Glasgow currently was. Since the death of Archbishop Boyd in 1581, James had been trying to place a highly unsuitable candidate, Robert Montgomerie, in the position. This the Kirk opposed and on 21 December 1585 the vacancy was filled by Thomas Erskine, cousin of the Earl of Mar. Crucially, the record of his appointment notes that all pensions granted on the Bishopric of Glasgow since Boyd's death were annulled.[15] On two grounds, therefore, the grant of Montgomerie's pension was illegal. Yet when the poet sailed off in 1586, the king still felt able to guarantee its continuation.

It was in March 1587 that James played his major card. It was then that he announced his intention of restoring to the see James Betoun, Archbishop under Mary and currently in France. Although broader political considerations lay behind the move, it did improve Montgomerie's situation. Inevitably it was unpopular. Betoun was a Catholic and in trying to supplant the staunchly Protestant Erskine with such a man, James openly flouted the Kirk and the Protestant Lords. It was also a move with complex legal implications. Sentence of "baratrie" (improper gaining of a benefice) and "foirfal-tour" (forfeiture) had been passed on Betoun in 1570 and on 12 February 1573 he had been denounced as a traitor.

To counter this the *Register of the Privy Council* appointing Betoun, specifically stated that the king had restored him "aganis the sentence of foirfaltour and baratrie given against him".

This last clause might at first sight not seem necessary, for under the later Acts of Pacification (1573) and Abolition (1585) a general pardon had been issued to those found guilty of such crimes. But in the second of these, Betoun had explicitly been named as an exception. The Privy Council wording shows an awareness of this, as does the Act of Ratification, passed in July 1587. There it was made clear that the only exceptions to the pardon were now those named in this later Act. Betoun, it seemed, was cleared. What appears to have been overlooked is the condition set out in both the Acts of Abolition and Pacification that their terms will apply only to those who accept the doctrines of the Reformed Church. The Act of Ratification failed to amend this and it was reaffirmed by the Act of Interpritatioun, passed in 1592, the very year in which Montgomerie's own case began. As a confirmed Catholic, Betoun was still unpardoned.

This was a very serious matter for Montgomerie, as his case depended largely on the acceptance of Betoun's right to restoration. In an anti-Catholic climate, fuelled by the recent affair of the Spanish blanks and with the judgment of the Act of Interpritatioun in front of them The Lords of Session had little option but to find against the poet. This they did, ruling in Erskine's favour on 13 July 1593.

This is to look at the evidence objectively. Montgomerie saw only the breach of a royal promise. Up to his imprisonment, his Catholic loyalties seem to me to have been subsidiary to his loyalty to James. Freed from that bond of friendship when the king failed to make any other provisions for his upkeep and presumably shunned him as one of those involved in the undercover negotiations with Spain, which had now become public knowledge, he became an even more fervent Catholic. It is probably after the judgment of 1593 that he encountered Duff. Certainly any journey to the Abbey at Würzburg postdated the trial, for the Latin poems place it after 1595, the date when the Scots took possession there.[16] The man described in these verses is the disillusioned 'ex-laureate', deprived of his high position at Court and embittered against the ruling Protestant powers. In such a situation, thoughts of a monastic retreat are wholly natural.

In fact, he spent his last years not under the strict régime of the Abbey but in exile in the West of Scotland. This period must have been one of deep frustration for an ambitious courtier, but it was not without its more convivial side. The self-portrait he paints in Sonnet 69 is of a Falstaff-like figure, drinking merrily among friends:

> I, Richie, Jane and George are lyk to
>   d[ee,]
> Four crabbit crippilis crackand in our   boasting;
>   crouch.   crouching place
> Sen I am trensh-man for the other   interpreter
>   thri[e,]
> Let drunken Pancrage drink to me in
>   D[utch.]

(S LXIX)

By this time he was suffering badly from the 'gravel' but was still ready to become involved in a Catholic plot, hatched by his friend Hugh Barclay of Ladyland and based in his native Ayrshire. Along with "some of the Montgomeries, Stewarts, Murrays and others",[17] Ladyland seized the small island of Ailsa Craig in the Firth of Clyde and fortified it in order to aid the rebellion of the Earl of Tyrone in Ireland. The venture was revealed to the authorities by the Protestant minister, Andrew Knox, and although Montgomerie may have been too ill to take a very active part, his involvement is certain, for he was ordered to appear before the Privy Council to answer charges. He did not attend and was officially outlawed on 14 July 1597.[18]

Recent work, developing on an obscure footnote of which most scholars were unaware, has established that little more than a year later the poet was dead.[19] The circumstances surrounding his funeral are of interest because they reflect the divided loyalties caused by a man who was both an outlawed Catholic and a highly respected poet. James himself gives a hint of the confusion:

> Though to his buriall was refused the
>   bell
> The bell of fame shall aye his praises
>   knell.

(II, 108)

Duff confirms this, adding that the wishes of the Calvinist ministers were ignored; that the Catholic nobility ("pia nobilitas") and the people urged the king to intervene, so that finally a proper burial with a royal cortège ("regali comitatu") was allowed.

John Durkan has now shown that much of this evidence is consolidated by contemporary records. On 22 August the Presbytery of Edinburgh ordered the bailies of the Canongate to "ansuer for bureing of umquhill Alexander Montgomerie poet, a papist, in thair kirk contrare the actis of the generall assemblie".[20] A week later the meeting took place. The bailies advanced the unlikely defence that they had not known the poet to be a Catholic. This was not accepted and they were "scharplie rebukit". Later a visitation was sent to Holyrood and once more profound dissatisfaction was expressed concerning the Canongate burial. The detailed account of these events suggests that Montgomerie had been buried in the kirk itself, not in the burial ground outside; that James had indeed intervened and that his action found some measure of popular support.

There are several paradoxes implicit in this situation. A man whose latest major act had been support for a Catholic rebellion is buried in a Protestant kirk. A poet who, during his later career, lost the open friendship of the king has that friendship powerfully demonstrated after death. An outlaw whose life was free for the taking dies amidst popular acclaim. But a still greater paradox remains. It centres not round Montgomerie's death and reputation then but around his reputation and writings now. At a time when critics of Scottish literature have freed themselves from the myth that only Burns and Scott are worthy of attention, Montgomerie still remains a relatively unknown figure in spite of his work's quality and variety. It is hoped that this short book may go some way towards redressing this major remaining injustice to the "Laureato materni" (laureate in the mother tongue).[21]

NOTES

1. *The Poems of King James VI of Scotland*, ed. James Craigie, 2 vols., STS, 1955, 1958. All quotations are based on this text.
2. Document in *The Poems of Alexander Montgomerie* (Supplementary Volume), ed. George Stevenson, STS, 1910, Appendix D, I. See also Scottish Record Office, *Eglinton Munimenta* GD/3/1, Bundle 76 No. 1, 23/4/1589.
3. Mark Dilworth, "New Light on Alexander Montgomerie", *The Bibliotheck*, IV, 1965, pp. 230–5; H. M. Shire, "Alexander Montgomerie. The oppositione of the court to conscience . . ." *Studies in Scottish Literature*, III, 1966, pp. 144–50.
4. Dilworth, *op. cit.*, p. 231.
5. Stevenson, *op. cit.*, p. 265; Shire, *Song, Dance and Poetry of the Court of Scotland under King James VI*, Cambridge, 1969, p. 85.
6. Stevenson, *op. cit.*, Appendix D, III, IV.
7. It is unlikely to refer to the poet himself as Cranstoun's punctuation suggests.
8. *Poems of James*, *op. cit.*, I, 81.
9. *Ibid.*, II, 120.
10. The metaphor appears in Montgomerie's 25th sonnet and elsewhere in Castalian writing.
11. Gordon Donaldson, *Scotland: James V to James VII*, Edinburgh and London, 1965, p. 189.
12. Stevenson, *op. cit.*, Appendix D, VI.

13. *Calendar of State Papers (Foreign)*, January–July 1589, p. 189, letter undated.
14. The documents covering the trial are in Stevenson, *op. cit.*, Appendix D, V–X.
15. The only exception is one "Nicoll Carnecross".
16. Dilworth, *op. cit.*, p. 232 (Poem II).
17. *Calendar of State Papers (Scottish)*, 1595–7, p. 568.
18. Stevenson, *op. cit.*, Appendix D, XI.
19. *The Percy Letters: the correspondence of Thomas Percy and David Dalrymple, Lord Hailes*, ed. A. F. Falconer, Binghampton, New York, 1954, p. 16n; John Durkan, "The Date of Alexander Montgomerie's Death", *Innes Review*, XXXIV, 1983, pp. 91–2.
20. Scottish Record Office, Edinburgh Presbytery Records ii CH2/121/2, 22/7/1598, unfoliated.
21. A title given to him by the author of the Latin version of *The Cherrie and the Slae*, his major poem.

CHAPTER II

PUBLIC AND DRAMATIC POETRY

Any ambitious young writer had to get his work known at Court, and the three poems which form the basis of this chapter were intended both for public entertainment and personal advancement. In them, Montgomerie submitted to the demands made by particular occasions but ensured that his audience would also know that they were being addressed by a poet whose linguistic and versifying skills were of the highest order.

The first two, 'The Navigatioun' and 'A Cartell of the Thre Ventrous Knights', are clearly part of an official celebration. They are possibly linked and belong to the early part of James's reign for, in the first, Scotland is described as a land

> Quhair presently beginneth for to ring   reign
> So sapient a ȝing and godly King.
>
> (MP XLVIII, 77–8)

1579 seems a likely composition date, for in October of that year James was officially welcomed into Edinburgh. The detailed accounts of this event, however, make no reference to performances of the sort suggested by Montgomerie's narrative, which may therefore have been used for a less lavish occasion such as the earlier entry into Holyrood or the Earl of Morton's reception at Dalkeith.

A first reading of 'The Navigatioun' might tempt one to dismiss it as being of more interest to the geographer than the literary critic. Using a fairly undemanding couplet form, the poet/narrator tells how he, in the company of three Eastern companions, a Turk, a Moor and an Egyptian, endures an eventful sea voyage to visit the

Scottish Court. Starting from Constantinople, they pass through the Hellespont into the Aegean Sea. They note with interest the site of Troy and then enter the Mediterranean, heading first for Rhodes and taking a route between Malta and Sicily. Despite storms they eventually reach the Gulf of Genoa in safety and from there progress up the coast of Aragon and Portugal before heading for Ireland. They pass the Channel Islands, come into the English Channel and travel along the eastern coast of England, finally arriving at Leith after weighing anchor at the Bass Rock.

Closer analysis reveals that the simple verse form and the broad sweep of the narrative are dictated by the dramatic nature of the piece. Montgomerie's words are an important but subsidiary part of a larger spectacle, being mounted to impress the teenage king. That is why the poet/narrator frequently calls on his audience to *look* at what is being presented; to note for example the exotic clothes worn by himself and his companions:

> As I my self and all the rest ȝe se
> From Turkie, Egypt and from Arabie.
> As for myself, I am ane German borne,
> Quha ay this fasion, whilk ȝe se, hes
>   worne.

style of clothing

(19–22)

It is also why the tale ends not with the port of Leith but an invitation to dinner and dancing:

> To shaw the way unto ȝour Grace's hall,
> Þat, eftir supper, we might sie the ball.

(273–4)

The entertainment is intended as a prelude to further socialising and aims at putting the guests in a relaxed mood.

It seems likely that apart from the contrasting and exotic

costumes, there was also a large model ship, which moved along as the various adventures were recounted. Certainly this was the case some fifteen years later at the baptism of the Prince of Wales. Then, William Fowler describes a more extravagant entertainment which employed "a most sumpteous, artificiall, and wel proportioned ship".[1] The vessel was 8 feet broad with a keel 18 feet long and a height, measured to the highest flag, of 40 feet. The sea was 24 feet long and the ship moved, apparently without external aid. It had guns of brass; silver gilt anchors and sails of double white taffeta, bearing witness to the scale of the endeavour and the interest of the king, whose "invention" lay behind much of the planning.

Montgomerie's detailed descriptions of the raising of the sails (lines 91–100) and of the sailors' activities during the storm (lines 181–198) would assume a new importance if they were a commentary accompanied by mime and there is no doubt that he was writing for a performance dominated by "rare shewes and singular inventions". It is for this reason he chose a fairly unobtrusive narrative mode, so that attention would not be deflected from the visual splendours. At the same time, he managed to impress in a variety of ways.

First of all he lets his audience know that he is capable of much more ambitious rhetorical feats. Embarking briefly on a discussion of the fate of Troy, which incidentally establishes his knowledge of classical literature, he pulls himself up:

> Sik Pleonasmus figurs I refuse:
> I shape a shorter Syncopa till use.
> And, to my purpose quicklie for to cum,
> We entred nixt in Mediterraneum.

(123–6)

He is restraining his rhetorical talents because of the laws of decorum. Yet even within these limits, he is free to

highlight moments of crisis, making effective use of
imagery and mythology:

overwhelmed   The cluds blak ou'rquhelmit all the
                               skyis.
began   Neptunus ryders begouth also to ryis;
                            The bowand Dolphin tumbland lyk a
                               whele,
                            Quharby our Maister understude right
                               wei[ll]
                            That Eolus wes kindling up in yre.

                                                               (183–7)

He also proves himself master of a range of dialogue,
assuming now the learned tones of the Eastern visitors and
now the more couthy voice of a "hartsum wyf" from Leith:

                            "Be blyth," quod sho, "for ȝe sall se our
                               king;
                            God blisse his Grace, and mak him long
reign   to ring."

                                                               (267–8)

   If he manages in these ways to convey his skill as a poet,
he also uses his position as actor/narrator[2] to tell the king
something of his own character. He is not only "German
borne" in the sense of being a colourfully dressed
representative of Europe, he is also "german" in the sense
of being related to the king. It is as a relative and therefore
a man of consequence that he welcomes James.
   His is also the voice of experience addressing youth. The
journey may be a fictitious one, but the poet has himself
"bene in mony cuntrey strange" and has direct experience
of long voyages. This gives his account greater weight and
allows him to assume the dual role of eulogiser and adviser
adopted by Alexander Scott and Richard Maitland when
earlier welcoming his mother to the throne.[3]
   The praise is fulsome. He calls attention to James's
wisdom and birth:

So sapient a ʒing and godly King,
A Salomon for richt and judgiment:
In eviry langage he is eloquent.
All lands about do beir of him record;
He is the chosen vessell of the Lord.

(78–82)

He conveys the enthusiasm of all people at home and
abroad for this gifted youth. Turks, Moors, Egyptians and
Germans worship him but so do the people on the Bass
Rock and the woman of Leith.

Nor is the eulogy confined to the present. It is given a
historical dimension for James is the inheritor of a proud
regal line whose origins, although variously defined, are
incontestably heroic. This is established when the Egyptian claims that Scottish kings are descended from the
Pharaohs while the Turk argues for Greek ancestry. The
poet takes no sides but concludes that James's noble
ancestry accounts for their having undertaken so long a
journey on his behalf.

If past and present combine to glorify the royal line of
Scotland, the immediate future may overshadow both, for
James could soon accede to the throne of England. Sur-
veying the English coast, the visitors again fall into discussion, this time considering the situation after Elizabeth
dies. The outcome, they decide, is in the hands of God but
the claim of the Scottish king is one of the strongest. The
narrator, addressing James directly, again sums up:

Syndrie wes sibbe, bot ay ʒour Grace wes nar.

(230)

Montgomerie, therefore, praises James through all the
human dimensions of time. But he also suggests an
allegoric interpretation which moves the praise on to a
higher level, beyond time. The story of three wise men
travelling from the east, guided by stars, to worship a king
echoes St Matthew's version of the Nativity. In so doing,
Montgomerie reinforces the claim to 'divine right' which

James espoused so fervently. God's ultimate control is stressed and restressed throughout the poem. Situations as varied as the safety of the ship, the fate of Constantinople and the English succession are all confidently referred to divine benevolence. By suggesting the parallel between Christ and James, Montgomerie pays his king the greatest compliment of all, for he is indeed "the chosen vessell of the Lord", raised by God above the rest of humanity and ultimately responsible to eternal powers.

If Montgomerie proves himself a skilful eulogiser, he is no less effective in the rôle of mature counsellor. Indeed the poem opens on a note of warning. A garden metaphor is used to advise the king of his vulnerability. He is a rose-bud threatened by "storme", "venemous beistis" and "weeds". Around him he must plant wise counsellors, trusted relatives and holy preachers. But above all he must school himself in scripture:

> Thy gardene wall mak the New Testament,
> So sall thou grow without impediment.
>
> (15–16)

This message is viewed from another angle when Montgomerie reminds his audience of Constantinople's fate. Founded in a spirit of pure Christianity, it was lost when its rulers gave way to vice. And in case James regards this tale of divine retribution merely as a digression, its relevance to his own case is spelt out:

> Let uther lands a mirrour of this mak,

neighbours

> And, by thair nichtbours, example let
>   thame tak.
>
> (49–50)

The older poet thus counsels his king in the manner approved by contemporary historians. Only by trusting in God, having wise advisers and learning the lessons of the past will the promise of the Nativity-based myth be fulfilled in the face of dangerous political reality.

'The Navigatioun' permits Montgomerie to present

himself variously as poet, entertainer, man of action, eulogiser and counsellor. The shorter 'Cartell' is, by comparison, a lighter piece, although the title does suggest that French verse and Ronsard in particular are already influencing the poet. Also its theme and techniques are so similar to the other work, that it seems likely either that it is part of the same entertainment or that the success of the one led Montgomerie to repeat the formula.

Once more the poet takes the position of actor/narrator and is accompanied by a trio of Eastern nobles. This time they are dressed for combat and he is similarly attired ("our clothing"). It may well be that he has forsaken the part of a German and is also meant to come from the east, because in the 'Flyting' his opponent contemptuously refers to his having 'blackened up' to introduce a "guyse" (masque).[4] The four have again endured a "perillous" voyage in search of the king and are to be part of an entertainment mounted in his honour. The emphasis is still on spectacle, so much so indeed, that Montgomerie apologises for delaying the action with verse:

> And mairatou'r, we come not to that   moreover
>   end
> To wery ȝou and wast the day in verse,
> Quhilk otherwyse we purpose for to
>   spend.
>
> (MP XLIX, 14–16)

This conventionally modest opening, as in 'The Navigatioun', reveals his awareness of the spoken word's minor rôle. But in fact much thought has gone into the 'making' of the poem. In particular Montgomerie has adopted the interlacing rhymescheme ABABBCBC, much favoured in sixteenth-century Scottish verse. It is a demanding form and in choosing it Montgomerie shows that interest in complex verse patterns which is to characterise much of his later work. Another feature which links the poem with earlier Scottish verse and will become a feature of the

'maister poete's' writing is the use of alliteration, here
increasing at moments of high drama:

> Quhilk for to sie, we saild by syndry
>   shoir[s,]
> And past the perillous gredy gulfe of
>   Perse,
> And levir sees that syndry shippis devoirs,
> Quhair is no fish bot monsters fell and
>   feirs[e].
>
> (9–12)

coagulated

In the 'Flyting', Montgomerie makes much heavier use
of alliteration and adopts more ambitious verse forms. But
in 'A Cartell', although these skills are introduced more
modestly, they do underline the artificiality of the piece.
This emphasis on literary artifice is important in another
way for the entertainment it heralds is also 'artificial'. The
three knights are not participating in serious jousting
but in chivalric games such as running at the ring. As
representatives of the East they will compete against
knights from the Scottish Court with victory going to the
group who are judged superior by the royal party. In other
circumstances, we are assured, they would not hesitate to
show their courage but this is a period of festivity when
chivalric games are more fitting, and the characteristics of
masque and tournament mingle.

Together the outdoor activities of 'A Cartell' and the
indoor spectacle of 'The Navigatioun' provide the same
mixture of courtly delights aimed at by Fowler and Lord
Lindores when making the arrangements for Prince
Henry's baptism.

> . . . those exercises, that wer to be used for decoration
> of that solemnitie were to be devided both in Feeld
> pastimes, with Martiall and heroicall exploites, and in
> houshold, with rare shewes and singular inventions.[5]

Just as the sumptuous ship formed the centre of the
'household' entertainment and recalls 'The Navigatioun',

so Fowler's 'Feeld' events have much in common with those anticipated by 'A Cartell', although again the scale is more extravagant. Three Turks, three Christian Knights of Malta, three Amazons and three Moors competed for two days in a variety of martial competitions, the winners being rewarded with a diamond ring presented by Queen Anne.

It is interesting that the linking of indoor and outdoor entertainments is considered desirable by Fowler and Lindores for it strengthens the likelihood that 'A Cartell' and 'The Navigatioun' formed separate parts of the same spectacle. Certainly Fowler's description of the field events also emphasises that they were primarily a dramatic spectacle. He refers to the contestants as "actours" and "gentlemen who . . . sustained these personages"; is always concerned to introduce "some noveltie to the beholders" and calls the whole event a "mask". The distinctions between reality and game, insisted on by Montgomerie, suggest that he saw 'A Cartell' in the same light. It was, like 'The Navigatioun', a performance, fittingly introduced by a leading poet and a suitable vehicle for drawing to the attention of the king his skills as a dramatic poet.[6]

He wrote one further poem which might have formed part of a public entertainment. That is the spirited lyric 'Hay! now the day dawis', which is set to a lively old tune and follows in a tradition of works using the same first line and verse form.[7] It contains a powerful description of knights preparing for contest:

> All curageous knichtis
> Aganis the day dichtis   prepare
> The breist plate that bright is
> To feght with thair fone.
> The stoned steed stampis   stallion
> Throu curage and crampis   prances
> Syn on the land lampis,   strides
> The night is neir gone.

(MP XLI)

But this is only part of a general view of varied dawn activities and the poem is more plausibly regarded as a lyric expressing youthful enthusiasm for the fullness and variety of life at Court.

The Flyting of Montgomerie and Polwart belongs to quite another tradition and was a later composition. It was written before *The Reulis and Cautelis*, so a date in the early 1580s seems certain. It too was an entertainment, but one in which the poet's art did not have to vie with scenic effects or miming. As suggested in Chapter One, the contestants indulged in a battle of name-calling and vituperation for the benefit of a courtly audience, who acted as judges. No insult was too offensive, no slander too outrageous for inclusion but the spirit was one of 'game' or of "generous emulation" as the unknown author of 'The Epistle to the Reader' informs us.[8]

Although flytings did have "a context in real life",[9] the literary traditions behind them are many and varied. Continental sources such as the Provençal 'débat' and 'jeu parti' or the invectives of the Italian humanist Poggio Bracciolini have been suggested as antecedents of the form in Scotland, as has the Gaelic 'aoir', a form of poetical invective originating in Ireland. But the most immediate analogue is the celebrated flyting at James IV's Court between Dunbar and Kennedy. Recently included in both the Bannatyne and Maitland MSS, this earlier contest may well have been known to Montgomerie and Polwart and inevitably the two works share a variety of features. To argue that the one is a source for the other on the grounds that words and phrases are shared, however, seems to me rather dangerous.[10] True, some of the parallels are unusual. The cry of "cor mundum" escaping from the lips of a supposedly penitent Dunbar is, for example, given by both Polwart and Montgomerie to their opponent in moments of imagined degradation. But the finite number of verbal insults available and the restrictions implied by heavy alliteration make echoing inevitable. Also, one of the aims of the 'game' is to be as ingenious as possible, so that if the earlier contest were known, later poets would strive to be as *different* as possible. In such a context it is safer not to urge too close a connection.

That said, it is clear that in each case the challenge was made by the less established poet (Kennedy; Montgomerie) to a writer who held the senior position at Court. Much is therefore made of Montgomerie's success in chasing Polwart from his coveted position at the "chimney nuike". The verses were read aloud in full Court as the Montgomerie MSS confirm, so forming another type of entertainment.[11] The detailed picking up of quite complex arguments, which is especially characteristic of the later contest, suggests either that the debate continued over a number of days or (more probably) that the contestants passed individual manuscript contributions on to their opponent, who then had time to consider his reply.

This leads naturally to a consideration of the major difference between the two flytings. It is not simply that the later one is longer nor that it involves three contributions from each poet as against two. Dunbar and Kennedy use the same stanza throughout (the Ballat Royal). They are free to indulge in all the usual rhetorical tricks of the flyter but they never depart from that form. Polwart and Montgomerie move from one type of stanza to another, making mastery of versification a major criterion in determining superiority. Variation of line length also permits greater experimentation with rhythm, internal rhyme and alliteration. They are free either to imitate the form chosen by their opponent, showing a more intricate use of it, or to adopt a more complex stanza, implicitly challenging the other to 'match that!'. In their invectives the skills of the 'makar' are much more ostentatiously displayed.

In such a context, the specific arguments advanced are probably of less importance than the manner in which they are presented, so my account of the debate will be a simplified one. Montgomerie's initial challenge relies heavily on animal comparisons (mouse; toad etc) and scurrilous namecalling ("cultron cuist"). These are the stock in trade of flytings and will recur throughout. But here they are used to emphasise Polwart's diminutive stature and subhuman behaviour. Such a creature cannot hope to match the writer in any form of utterance, let alone a poetic contest. In his reply, Polwart maintains the insults and animal metaphors but mounts a more specific personal attack on Montgomerie as man and poet. Unflattering references are made to his drunkenness, his Catholicism and to his appearance in masques. His earlier writings are "raggit roundaillis" composed at the insistence of foolish men. Above all, he has no ear for rhythm as his verse "haultis for fault of feit lyk myne".

These initial contributions are short—20 and 48 lines respectively. They are the poetic equivalent of throwing down the gauntlet. The battle begins in earnest when Montgomerie accuses Polwart of being a sheep-stealer:

barren ewe; hillock	For mony ʒeld ʒow thow cald fra ane know,
hollow; stole	And hid þame in ane how, stark theif, quhan þow staw þame.

(T, 67–8)

Condemned to death he pays his way out of difficulties but should eventually be hung for these crimes and another type of theft—plagiarism. He has stolen from David Lindsay and is "Chauceris cuik". He, rather than Montgomerie, writes unmetrically and so will be ousted from his privileged position in "þe kingis kitching nuik". Whatever his fate on earth he will end up among the devils in Hell.

In his reply Polwart specifically answers the double charge of theft. He dismisses the accusation of sheep-stealing, turning it back on his opponent. As for the claim that he is a plagiarist:

> Also I may be Chauceris ma[n]
> And [ȝet] thy maister not the les. (T, 159–60)

He is accepted as leading poet and scorns to match with
someone who cannot write metrically and uses poor
similes. Having countered the major points, he introduces
two new ideas. First, he relates Montgomerie's immediate
genealogy. Born of a devil and a dun cow, he was suckled
by a black sow in the midden. Then, feigning concern for
the poet's health, Polwart suggests a variety of fantastic
cures, which serve to highlight his 'patient's' ignorance
and devilishness.

Montgomerie's final contribution develops these ideas
in a highly imaginative manner while taking up where he
had left off with his opponent among devils. The birth of
Polwart, offspring of an elf and an ape, is set amongst
devilish rejoicings at Hallowe'en. In what is the finest
movement in the flyting, Montgomerie first sets the scene
in that court of Faery, which James was later to condemn
in his *Daemonologie* as an illusion "rifest in the time of
Papistrie".[12] In turn he describes the visitations of the
Fates, witches and apes, each confirming Polwart's
monstrous nature. As the devilish rejoicings reach their
climax, his opponent is finally consigned to eternal
darkness. Not content with outdoing Polwart's brief
genealogy, Montgomerie also provides for him a much
longer list of illnesses. For over sixty heavily alliterated
lines the "weird sisteris" (Fates) curse him with every
disease known to man. These include:

> The frenesie, the fluikis, the fykis and þe felt,   flux; itching of anus; gravel
>
> The feveris, the totteris with the spenȝie fleis,   staggers; spanish
>
> The doyt and the dysmell, indifferentlie delt,   brain disorder; melancholy
>
> The pelodie, the palsie, þe poikis lyk peis.   alopecia; pustules
>
> (T, 307–10)

Polwart's final offering is no anti-climax. By far the
longest contribution, it is divided into three sections. Of
these the first two focus on Montgomerie's appearance and
character respectively. The last strives for victory on two
levels. Rhetorically he tries to match the long list of
alliterating illnesses with a similar list of insults which
begins:

foolish; shit	Fond flytter, scheitt schytter, baccoun bytter, befyld!
bleater; one who impales paddocks on a spit	Blunt bleitter, padok speitter, pudding eitter, perverss!

(T, 761–2)

Dialectically he sums up the argument and scores some
neat debating points, ending on a note of supreme
confidence:

fetter-defiler	Lik butter, throt cutter, fisch gutter, fyl
	    þe fetter!
	Cum bleitand, and greitand and eitand
	    thy letter.

(T, 830–1)

Final victory, we know, went to Montgomerie, but the
judges did not have an easy task. Polwart may have been
removed from the "chimney nuik" but he does not reveal
himself as an unworthy tenant. Let us imagine ourselves
listening to the debate and evaluating it in turn against
three criteria: rhetorical and versifying skills; debating
ability; and poetic imagination.

Both writers leave their most complex verse forms to the
end and Montgomerie in particular makes each succeeding stanza more intricate than the one that preceded it. He
starts with a lively quatrain using internal rhyme and
repeated phrases:

	Polwart, ye peip like a mouse amongst thornes,
nowledge	Na cunning ye keip, Polwart ye peip:

Ye looke like a sheip and ye had twa
    hornes,
Polwart, ye peip like a mouse amongst
    thornes.

(H, 1–4)

When assessing *The Flyting* for possible inclusion in his
Reliques, Bishop Percy thought this movement the best,
because none "of the other pieces (were) so spirited",[13] and
certainly it provides a striking opening. Next, Montgomerie adopts an eight-line stanza, interlacing his rhymes
not only at the end but in the middle as well. Finally he
moves to a thirteen-line stanza of almost unbelievable
complexity. A four-stress pattern based on the anapaest,
but with syllabic variation, governs the first nine lines
while the last four consist of three iambic tetrameters and a
trimeter. Heavy alliteration and a demanding rhyme
scheme provide further constraints. This is the stanza
which especially impressed King James and his critical
instincts did not let him down when he isolated the lines
describing Polwart's fantasy-birth:

Into the hinderend of harvest, on ane
    alhallow evin,
Quhen our goode nichtbouris ryddis, if I   neighbours
    reid richt,
Sum buklit on ane bunwyd and sum on   fixed firmly; stalk of
    ane bene,   ragwort; beanstalk
Ay trippand in trowpis fra the twie-
    licht;
Sum saidlit ane scho aip all grathit into   arrayed
    grene,
Sum hobling on hempstaikis, hovand on   hempstalks; remaining
    hicht.   stationary
The king of pharie with þe court of the
    elph quene,
With mony alrege incubus, ryddand   weird
    that nicht.

wicked person	Thair ane elph and ane aip, ane unsell begate
place near Edinburgh	In ane peitpot by Powmathorne
brat; bush	That brachart in ane buss wes borne;
	They fand ane monstour on the morne,
worse looking than	War facit nor ane cat.[14]

(T, 268–80)

Here all the skills of the makar are on show, mastery over complex rhythms, rhymes, patterns of alliteration and, above all, over a vast vocabulary spilling on to the page with an enthusiasm anticipating Sir Thomas Urquhart.

But many of Polwart's stanzas are almost as complex and his final list of insults exhibits a 'fouth' of words, just as impressive as Montgomerie's. If I award the judgment on this level to the latter, it is by a small margin and this bears witness to the high standards of professionalism among the leaders of the Castalian band. When it comes to assessing their debating powers, my own award would go to Polwart. He is at all times careful to counter the exact points raised by his opponent. His first reply seizes at once on the two charges of theft, answers them and returns them with interest before advancing to new indictments of his own. Montgomerie does not sidestep major issues but he is not so painstaking. Also, Polwart has the last word and takes advantage of this to make some telling points about the Ayrshire poet's repetitiveness and inconsistencies of argument. He also claims with some justification that descent from an ape (Montgomerie's claim about him) is not so damning as the fiendish genealogy he had invented.

The debating element in the poem is not unimportant and Polwart would probably have made a better lawyer than Montgomerie. In the end, however, the contest is not a legal but a poetic one and it is in the use of the poetic imagination to establish atmosphere and depict vivid dramatic moments that Montgomerie stands supreme. In particular his last contribution with its eerily comic account of the forces of darkness is fit to rank with Burns's 'Tam o' Shanter'. Here too his dramatic training pays dividends for his use of dialogue is particularly impressive, as is his knowledge of mythology, astronomy and the folklore of 'faery'. All combine when the witches at Polwart's 'baptism' deliver him into the hands of Mahoun:

> Be þe moving of þe mone,
>   mapamone, & þe kingis ell,   globe; belt of Orion
> Be Phlegitoun, the sevin starnis and þe   Phlegethon;
>   Chairlwane,   Plough
> Be the hicht of þe heavin and lawnes of
>   hell,
> Be all the brether of Beliallis buird in   council
>   ane band,
> Be the pollis, þe planeittis and singis all   poles; signs;
>   twell,   twelve
> Be þe michtis of þe moone—lat mirknes
>   remane—
> Be the elementis [all] that our craft can
>   compell,
> Be the floodis infernall and fureis of
>   pane,
> Be all the ghaistis of our gang, that
>   dwellis þair doun,
>   In signe of Stikis, that stinking strand,   Styx
>   And Pluto, that our court command,
>   Resave this harlot of our hand,
>   In name of Mahoun.
>
>   (T, 437–49)

Polwart could not match such versatility and in the early 1580s the Court had, deservedly, a new 'laureate'.

NOTES

1. *The Works of William Fowler*, ed. Henry W. Meikle, 3 vols., STS, II, 1936, p. 190.
2. In *The Flyting of Montgomerie and Polwart*, Polwart refers to Montgomerie taking part in a "guyse" or masque. (See Note 4.) Internal evidence from both 'The Navigatioun' and 'A Cartell' also supports the view that the poet was actively involved in the performances.
3. R. D. S. Jack, "Mary and the Poetic Vision," *Scotia*, III, 1979, pp. 35–7.
4. Stevenson, *op. cit.*, p. 134.
5. Fowler, *op. cit.*, II, 172.
6. For the argument that he also wrote a play, see M. P. McDiarmid, "*Philotus*: a play of the Scottish Renaissance," *Forum for Modern Language Studies*, III, 1967, pp. 223–35.
7. See *The Gude and Godlie Ballatis*, ed. A. F. Mitchell, STS, 1897, p. 192.
8. *The Poems of Alexander Montgomerie*, ed. James Cranstoun, STS, 1887, p. 57.
9. Priscilla Bawcutt, "The Art of Flyting," *Scottish Literary Journal*, X, 1983, p. 8.
10. Rudolf Brotanek, *Untersuchungen über das Leben und die Dichtungen Alexander Montgomeries*, Wien, 1896.
11. Rev. George Hill, *The Montgomery MSS (1603–1706)*, Belfast, 1869, p. 400.
12. *Minor Prose Works of King James VI and I*, ed. James Craigie, STS, 1982, p. 51.
13. *The Percy Letters, op. cit.*, p. 16.
14. *Poems of James, op. cit.*, I, 81. His version differs from that of Tullibardine. See Preface and Chapter VI.

CHAPTER III

THE LYRIC

i

THE KER MANUSCRIPT: Almost all the lyrics which can certainly be ascribed to Montgomerie, along with 'The Navigatioun', 'A Cartell', some epitaphs and a large group of sonnets are to be found in this quarto MS of 163 pages written in a neat and legible hand.[1] It is one of those gifted to Edinburgh University by William Drummond but has been given the name Ker because there is a signature, 'Margaret Ker', in a different hand on the flyleaf.

Dating is difficult but those poems which can definitely be assigned, through internal evidence, to a known event show that the collection covers a wide chronological range stretching from the late 1570s until a short time before the poet's death. The major question is whether the MS can also be dated before 1598 or whether, as most editors and critics believe, it belongs to the early seventeenth century. In the first case, of course, Montgomerie may himself have been responsible for the ordering. He may even have been the scribe. In the second no such authorial authority can be assumed.

At first sight the dilemma appears to have been solved by the presence of DP VII 'Away! vane world, bewitcher of my hairt' towards the end of the collection for it appeared *after* Montgomerie's death, accompanying Elizabeth Melvil's *Ane Godlie Dreame*. This rather uninspired work was first printed in 1603, so, the argument goes, Ker must belong to a later date. The simplicity of this conclusion has always troubled me. 'Away! vane world' is the only poem which seems to fall into this category. Elsewhere in the MS

the few works composed by writers other than Montgomerie are almost always given titles which reveal this
fact and they all pre-date his death. Why, therefore, in a
MS devoted to Montgomerie's work should the scribe
draw in a single lyric written by a minor poet after his
death and conceal the fact?

I think there is an answer to this last question and overall
I am inclined to accept that this is the situation. But I do so
with no certainty and aware of another possibility. It was
not uncommon in the sixteenth and seventeenth centuries
for a longer poem to be printed along with a much shorter
poem or song whose theme confirmed that of the major
work. *Ane Godlie Dreame* urges man to turn away from
worldly values and embrace Christ as does 'Away! vane
world'. And although the *Dreame* is twice directly
attributed to Melvill, 'Away! vane world' is not. It is
merely called "A comfortabill song"—i.e. a work which
may bring (further) comfort. The manuscript and printed
versions are not identical and all the variations in the latter
bring the argument more closely into line with that of the
Dreame. Elizabeth Melvill's own work is pedestrian; her
metres are often suspect and the 'comfortabill song' is
much superior to the title-poem which accompanies it.
Finally, 'Away! vane world' helps to fill out two pages
within the gathering, which would otherwise have
contained only eight lines of the *Dreame*. Scottish
printers did occasionally fill such unsightly gaps by
inserting another work by an established author.[2] It may
be that a version of Montgomerie's song was used for this
purpose, the printer being careful nowhere to claim it as
Melvill's.

On balance, however, I think it more likely that the
poem is Melvill's. In deciding this, I have been influenced
by the short religious poem which appears on the front
page of the MS. This page shows the effects of time more
than the rest of Ker and much of the lyric is illegible. But it
is, despite the presence of one uncharacteristic antique 'h'

form, in the same hand as that responsible for the MS as a whole and its theme, though conventional enough, is particularly apposite as an introduction to the work of a poet whose life was suddenly cut short. In appealing that we praise the Lord while fearing Him, the poet gives us only one reason. Such is God's power:

> That (He) may cut of at his vintage
> The breath of Princes.

It is particularly fitting, and surely more than coincidence, that such a verse introduces the work of James's "prince of Poëts",[3] a man who died in his prime and who, in his later years especially, turned to the comfort of religion.

If this is accepted, then the scribe or whoever was responsible for collecting the poems, did so shortly after Montgomerie's death and was acquainted with his history. Close study of the MS allows us to go further than this and conclude that he knew the poet's work well and almost certainly had access to his papers. Paradoxically this intimate knowledge reveals itself most clearly in those instances where he includes poems composed by other writers. These fall into two divisions. First, there are those where the heading (e.g. 'Ladyland to Cap. A. Mont-gomerie') makes it clear that they have been intentionally included. Here the poems are drawn in because they are necessary to complete a debate or discussion involving the 'maister poete' or, in one case, to provide a comment on the outcome of his petition to a fellow-writer. Only access to original papers or first-hand knowledge of the situation can account for their appearance. Elsewhere there is a sonnet which appears without attribution but is in fact simply a rendering in Scots of a sonnet by Constable. In this context we must remember that writers of this time (Wyatt and Drummond of Hawthornden are other examples) might include in their MSS poems which took their fancy, making only the slightest of alterations. The Constable sonnet, 'Thyne ee the glasse whare I beheld my

hairt', is one such and its inclusion once more suggests that
the scribe was working from the poet's own papers.

The ordering of the poems further confirms this while
providing a possible answer to the question posed earlier
about 'Away! vane world'. While the collection is not
broken up into neat thematic sections, some organising is
evident, and it is thematic rather than chronological. Most
obviously, the Manuscript has been arranged so that
religious lyrics open and close it. This is the outer circle.
Within it, the seventy sonnets also open on a devotional
note and end with a work scorning this world's values. The
effect in each case is to place the predominantly melancholy love poetry and the bitter biographical complaints
within a frame, which refers their argument to higher
ideals. The introductory religious lyric is consistent with
this attempt to present Montgomerie's work in a way
which would doubtless have pleased him, reflecting as it
does the religious fervour of mature years. 'Away! vane
world', as we shall see, forms part of this devotional frame
and may well have been 'borrowed' in order to confirm the
pattern, especially as the 'worldly' verse far outnumbers
the 'spiritual'.

If we must assume that this arrangement reflects scribal
rather than authorial intention, it is equally safe to assume
that the shorter groups or mini-sequences which have a
clear thematic or narrative unity and are sometimes given
separate numbering, are presented just as Montgomerie
ordered them. This feature will be discussed more fully in
the chapter devoted to the sonnet. But some groups of
religious, biographical and love lyrics are also set off one
from the other.

Considerations such as these have dictated my means of
approach to Montgomerie's lyrics. In the analysis which
follows I shall briefly call attention to the overall pattern
but assume authorial support for the arrangement only of
the mini-sequences. A discussion of general characteristics
will precede a more detailed analysis of those lyrics

concerned with love, the poet's own biography and religion. In this it will be noted that Occasional verse has been ignored. This is because James had advocated the sonnet as the form most adapted for particular comment on events at court. Within the Ker MS, only 'Now the day dawis' (which has been considered elsewhere) and a welcome to Lord Semple, which divides its praise between that gentleman and the poet's own bravery in overcoming illness, can be seen as Occasional pieces. For the Castalian band, the lyric usually had other functions.

ii

THE LYRIC: GENERAL: Montgomerie's lyrics are set firmly within the courtly tradition. He is in this sense the natural successor to Dunbar, Lindsay and Alexander Scott. But in his youth he had seen the Court and the houses of the nobles lose their position as centres for cultural entertainment in the bitterness of civil conflict. This is what Richard Maitland regrets, when he asks:

> Quhair is the blythness that hes bein
> Bayth in burgh and landwart sein,   country
> Amang lordis and ladyis schein   bright
> Daunsing, singing, game and play?[4]

And this is what James VI strove to re-create in the early years of his reign. As his *Reulis and Cautelis* are aimed at producing a new lyrical revival and as Montgomerie is the main model for this revival, it is helpful to relate the 'maister poete's' practice to some of the theoretical precepts laid down by his monarch.

James's treatise is first and foremost a handbook of rhetoric and versification. It devotes seven out of its eight chapters to techniques of writing verse and throughout the emphasis is on skilful literary craftsmanship. Montgomerie, as the study of *The Flyting* demonstrated, was firmly committed to this sort of mannerism and the first thing which impresses the student is the range of complex stanzas employed and the demanding rhyme schemes to which he submits himself:

> Lyk as the dum
> Solsequium
> With cair ou'rcum
> And sorow when the sun goes out of sight
> Hings down his head
> And droups as dead
> And will not spread
> But louks his leavis throu langour of the
>   nicht,
> Til folish Phaeton ryse
> With whip in hand
> To cleir the cristall skyis
> And light the land;
> Birds in thair bour
> Luiks for that hour
> And to thair prince ane glaid good-
>   morow givis,
> Fra thyn that flour
> List not to lour
> Bot laughis on Phoebus lowsing out his
>   leivis.
>   (MP XV, 1–18)

closes — But louks his leavis throu langour of the nicht,

freeing — Bot laughis on Phoebus lowsing out his leivis.

In this example, which is by no means the most involved,[5] the various restraints of rhyme and alliteration do not impede the simple story line. This is one of Montgomerie's finest qualities as a lyricist. Virtuoso stylistic techniques do not become an end in themselves, and this is so even when he is using the most extravagant of internal rhymes:

> In prison sen 3e hald my hairt,
> Releiv my smart; draw out this darte
> Furth of my bailfull breist.
> Haif pitie on my painfull parte.

As by the carte men knowes the arte,   map
Both south, north, west and eist,
3e may persave my wounds ar grene,
I say, and look bot to my ene.

(MP XLIV, 17–24)

Other Castalians, anxious to impress through stylistic
novelty, often sacrificed content to form. Montgomerie
with his intelligent use of enjambement, dramatic pauses
and transitions from direct to indirect speech knew how to
keep the balance and guide the speaking or singing voice
carefully onwards.

In terms of rhetoric his greatest debt is to the 'grands
rhétoriqueurs' in France. The last quotation, in which the
caesura rhymes both with the end of its own line and with
the immediately preceding one, combines two popular
French forms, 'rime renforcée' and 'rime batelée'. Lois
Borland has given us further evidence of his interest in this
school[6] and certainly no reader of the *Reulis and Cautelis*
could be surprised at this discovery. After all, in composing
it, James had been influenced by Du Bellay's *Deffense et
Illustration de la Langue Françoyse* and uses literary termi-
nology of French derivation. English writers and traditions
were not ignored but Esmé Stewart had turned the king's
attention across the Channel to the Pléiade and James's
own early verse shows a marked preference for Du Bartas,
Desportes and Saint Gelais.

Montgomerie almost certainly anticipated this tend-
ency but reading or listening to the senior poet's work,
the king must have observed two things in particular.
Although the example of the 'rhétoriqueurs' lay behind his
lyrical verse, his two favoured authors were Marot and
Ronsard, both of whom profited from the enormous
metrical range of their predecessors but, in their comparative "simplicity of execution",[7] broke with the very
tradition they in part espoused. The one was the major
precursor of the Pléiade, the other its most brilliant

product. In using Montgomerie's versè to point the way
forward for Scottish letters, James knew that he was
highlighting the work of a poet already committed to the
newest ideals of the European Renaissance.

Secondly, James saw that his 'maister poete', while
respecting tradition and being keen to imitate not only
French but also English and even (perhaps) Spanish
authors, valued his own voice above them all. Particular
source studies show that almost always he tried to adapt his
material in an original way. The two Marot adaptations,
which probably pre-date *The Reulis*, show the value placed
by the poet on his powers of 'invention'.

'The Elegie' is based on Marot's third *Elegie* but
seventeen additional lines show Montgomerie ingeniously
expanding on his model. A similar relationship exists
between 'A bony "No" ' and Marot's 'De Ouy et Nenny'.

> A bony "No" with smyling looks agane
> I wald ȝe leirnd, sen they so comely ar.
> As touching "ȝes," if ȝe suld speik so
>   plane,
> I micht reprove ȝou to haif said so far.
> Noght that ȝour grant in ony wayis
>   micht gar
> Me loth the fruit that Curage ocht to
>   chuse,
> Bot I wald only haif ȝou seme to skar
> And let me tak it, fenȝeing to refuse.
>   (MP XLII, 1–8)

make

be frightened

> Ung doulx Nenny avec ung doulx
>   soubzrire
> Est tant honneste; il le vous fault
>   apprendre.
> Quand est d'Ouy, si veniez à le dire,
> D'avoir trop dit je vouldrois vous
>   reprendre;

Non que je soys ennuyé d'entreprendre
D'avoir le fruict dont le desir me poingt;
Mais je vouldrois qu'en le me laissant
     prendre
Vous me dissiez: non, vous ne l'aurez
     point![8]

"Bony" and "comely" for "doulx" and "honneste"
suggest a less courtly context and the last two lines have
been reframed to prevent the blunt reporting of the lady's
reply. But this is imitation of the closest kind. The
'invention' lies in Montgomerie having composed two
additional stanzas, the first explaining the lover's motiva-
tions and the second converting particular experience into
proverbial advice for all—'Flie whylome love, and it will
folow thee."

So Marot's courtly epigram is given a less rarefied
setting and a wider application. Often Montgomerie will
do this—work within a courtly mode but produce an
original vision which in some ways joins the virtues of
courtly and popular. And although he honours the
principle of Imitation, he does so in order that his
Invention may be the more clearly highlighted. Thus his
practice once more confirms James's theory:

> Bot sen Invention is ane of the cheif vertewis in a
> Poete, it is best that ȝe invent ȝour awin subject ȝour
> self, and not to compose of sene subjectis.[9]

Of course it is inevitable that James's *Reulis* will provide
a good guide to Montgomerie's practice, given that the
royal author admired him so much. At the same time,
Montgomerie—dependent on royal patronage—would
later, like all the Castalians, heed the king's 'cautelis' and
obey his 'reulis' with pragmatic alacrity. In later years he
even wrote regretfully of having given exaggerated praise
to James's *Uranie*. That said, his accepted position as poetic
leader did give him more freedom than most and he never

really allowed James's position as Maecenas to interfere with his originality. A study of three further aspects of his lyrical verse will confirm this.

In the Preface to *The Reulis*, James is anxious to establish that he is leading not only a Scottish but a specifically vernacular revival. This was the period when he bitterly accused Buchanan of teaching him Latin to the detriment of Scots. Therefore he urges that new guidance in rhetorical practice is needed because the old rules drawn from classical and medieval verse are inadequate for the new works to be written in Scots. But one does not escape from one's conditioning as easily as this and frequent echoes of Ovid and Virgil, complex Latinate syntax and a heavy reliance on classical mythology all betray the bias of the king's education.

Montgomerie was not unacquainted with classical writing and in his verse too we can detect the influence of Virgil, Tibullus and (especially) Ovid. Yet this learning is worn lightly and seldom dominates the poetic argument. If, as rhetorician, he was less extravagant than Stewart of Baldynneis or William Fowler, his muted classicism is highlighted when we compare his unobtrusive use of classical mythology with the heavyhanded pedestrian techniques of James or Alexander Craig. In the following example he skilfully draws in the story of Echo and Narcissus to support an amorous complaint:

> Som thing, Echo, thou hes for to rejose
> Suppose Narcissus some tyme the
>   forsook.
> First he is dead, syne changed in a rose
> Quhom thou nor nane hes power for to
>   brook.
> Bot, be the contrair, evirie day I look
> To sie my love attraptit in a trane
> From me, Echo, and nevir come agane.
>   (MP VII, 36–42)

snare

The stanza is once again drawn from the grands rhétori-
queuers but the colloquial tone, the tripping metre and the
use of an episodic narrative mode combine to remove any
impression of forced erudition.

Two other traditions combine to confirm the lightness of
touch and directness of message, which are so successfully
counterpointed against demanding verse forms and
extravagant rhetorical devices. The first of these is the
musical revival. The Court of Mary had made musicians
welcome and encouraged a variety of modes (mainly
French). James, although he was not himself musically
gifted, continued his mother's policy, strengthening the
Chapel Royal and encouraging men of the calibre of
Blackhall and the Hudson brothers to associate themselves
with the Castalians.

As the researches of Elliott and Shire have proved, at
least thirty of Montgomerie's lyrics were given musical
settings.[10] It seems likely that at least in some instances he
worked in close collaboration with the composers. If we
accept this, two points immediately emerge. Once more he
is working within a courtly tradition, for native airs were
not popular and a clear distinction was made between
them and courtly songs. Once more, the major tradition
was French and the minor one English.[11] But whether his
lyrics are set to an elaborate chanson arising from the
influence of the dance on the contrapuntal tradition (e.g.
'In Throu the windoes of myn ees') or to a simpler
harmonic song (e.g. 'Adeu, O desie of delyt') his bias is still
towards the popular. Light tripping metres and long/short
line alternations characterise many of these lyrics. 'The
Solsequium', earlier cited, is a particularly good example.
A pure part song in sixteenth-century French style, it soon
became a favourite at court and beyond, encouraging
Montgomerie to compose seventeen religious lyrics in the
same stanza pattern.

Sometimes too the musical settings reflect this popular
bias, although here the degree of Montgomerie's influence

(or even its existence) must remain in doubt. 'Adeu O desie of delyt', for example, has a very complex setting, with "the two inner voices crossing one another so frequently that they cannot be said to be merely functional parts".[12] Yet Elliott has shown that a round is related to the part song, giving evidence of one aspect of 'freeman's music' with its blend of courtly and popular elements. Some religious lyrics too are set to airs which, although ultimately courtly in derivation, are nonetheless simple and unaffected. One such is the triumphant song which ends the Ker MS. Here Montgomerie makes sure that the words and ideas will reinforce that joyous simplicity:

> Come, my Childrene dere draw neir me,
> To my Love when that I sing.
> Mak ȝour ears and hairts to heir me
> For it is no eirthly thing
> Bot a Love
> Far above
> Other loves all, I say,
> Which is sure
> To indure
> When as all things sal decay.
>
> (DP VIII, 1–10)

The musical dimension is of great importance and available evidence suggests that Montgomerie took an active and informed interest in this side of the Castalian Renaissance. Once more he works within courtly traditions but in a way which brings to those traditions a freshness and directness characteristic of all his finest work.

Perhaps the study of this fruitful tension between courtly and popular is most neatly concluded by looking at a comparatively minor aspect of his art—his use of proverbs. These form a powerful leitmotiv in his verse. They may be used as a refrain reinforcing the lyric's primary message, as in 'A Counsell against dispair in Love', where the reader is consistently urged to "Drie furth the inch as thou hes done the span"; one may be introduced only to be trumped by another as in stanza 4 of 'A Descriptione of Vane Lovers'; or a whole series may be grouped together providing variations on a single theme:

> For I haif hard in adagies of auld,
> That tyme dois waist and weir all things
>   away;
> Then trow the taill that treu men oft hes
>   tauld—
> A turne in tyme is ay worth other tway.
> Siklyk I haif hard oft-tymis suith men
>   say,
> That negligence зit nevir furtherit nane;
> Als, seindle tymis luck folowes long   few
>   delayis.
> Tak tyme in tyme, or tyme will not be
>   tane.   (MP I, 9–16)

This almost obsessive concern with proverbs shows once again his love of popular wisdom. People outwith the Court circle would understand such verses were they ever given the opportunity of hearing them. But in using them the 'maister poete' is still observing courtly rules, for Molinet had advocated them as a means of clinching a stanza and even James had given them a place in his *Reulis*: "They man be proper for the subject, to beautifie it, chosen in the same forme as the Comparisoun."[13]

Montgomerie is therefore recognisably a man of his time and has the Court poet's interest in past traditions and earlier writers. Yet in his best work he usually looks forward, handling those traditions imaginatively and choosing to model himself on authors with similar innovative aims. Like most early Castalians he was drawn primarily to French models, for there was a stated desire to distinguish Scots writing from English, but that did not imply an unhealthy ignoring of work produced south of the border. Ronsard and Marot may have been preferred but

Watson and Constable were also read and appreciated. Above all, he tried to match his Renaissance enthusiasm for rhetorical and stanzaic complexity with the more direct and 'popular' tendencies I have analysed. In so doing he found a unique and powerful voice which dominated Scottish poetry for over two decades.

iii

LOVE LYRICS: The vast majority of Montgomerie's love lyrics belong to the later Petrarchist tradition as developed by that writer's followers in Italy, France and England. They therefore seem very similar to other amorous lyrics of the period, even if the various 'simplifying' tendencies discussed above do give them some degree of autonomy.

True to this tradition, Montgomerie sees himself as one coming late to love, who, for that reason, finds the fall into servility even more painful. He can only repent and hope that his anguish may find mercy from the lady:

been negligent

> Quhair I haif reklest, I recant;
> In tymes to cum I promise to be true.
> Laith wes I to begin, I grant,
> To love—bot now my reklesnes I rue.

(MP XXIII, 31–4)

Like Petrarch and the Petrarchists he dramatises the moment by attributing his downfall to Cupid, who has been waiting vengefully on the sidelines hoping to catch a proud defier of his laws. Once sure of his quarry, the god fires his arrow and the luckless boaster finds himself fatally wounded:

> Upon my feet incontinent I start,
> And stagring stood, astonisht with the

blow

> straik.
> Haiv pitie thairfoir on my painfull harte
> And saif the man that suffers for ȝour
> sa[ik.]

(MP XXXIII, 21–4)

This quotation is taken from the dream vision, 'Quhen folish Phaeton had his course outrun'. It leads directly into another Petrarchan convention—that love enters first through the eyes and then attacks the heart:

> My harte wes ay at libertie till now
> That I did sie ȝour cumly cristall ene,
> Quhais luifsum looks so peirc't my body thr[ou,]
> That, ay sensyn, ȝour bondman I haif   afterwards
> be[ne.]

(MP XXXIII, 25-8)

The figure of Cupid and the eyes/heart conceit recur frequently in Montgomerie's love lyrics. The god's various powers and the poetic implications of losing one's heart are sometimes ingeniously developed but that ingenuity has been anticipated by early writers within the tradition. The many comparisons between the Lady and the sun may be seen in the same way, as can the detailed analyses of the lover's despair and his illogical desire to court death through love. Indeed, this last symptom becomes, in a wider context, but one of the many paradoxes which define the Petrarchan passion:

> Evin dead behold I breath!
> My breath procures my pain,
> Els dolour eftir death
> Suld slaik when I war slane:
> Bot Destinies disdane
> So span my fatall threid,
> But mercy to remane
> A martyr quik and deid.   alive
> O fatall deidly feid!   feud
> O Rigour but remorse!
> Since thair is no remeid,
> Come Patience, perforce.

(MP XX, 1–12)

The stoicism contemplated in the last line is yet another
feature which Montgomerie's verse shares with that of the
Petrarchists. For Petrarch himself it had been associated
with Laura's semi-divine status. Except in moments of
deepest despair, the poet was reconciled to his lot because
he knew that adoration of an unattainable but perfect lady
was preferable to a series of successful love affairs with lesser
women. Montgomerie and most of the later European
Petrarchists do not stress the lady's spiritual qualities but
do urge the need to persevere. Characteristically, in 'A
Counsell against Dispair in Love', he reinforces the idea
through a proverbial refrain:

> Quhat meins thou now fra thou be in
>   her waird?
> Thy libertie, alace! it is to lait.
> . . . .
> With patience persaiv thy awin estait:
> Drie furth the inch as thou hes done the
>   span.

keeping (gloss for *waird*)
endure (gloss for *Drie*)

(MP VII, 9–10, 15–16)

When the immediate problems of unrequited love lead
him into philosophic contemplation he may see this
patience as a reason for granting him salvation ('Ressave
this harte, whois constancie wes sik'); or the very power of
passion may cause him to wonder whether there is any
divine force which can contain it ('The Secret Prais of
Love'). What he does not emphasise is Petrarch's belief in
temporal love as a means to divine charity; the lady as
'ladder to God'. This confirms my view that Italian ideas
are reaching him at second hand through French or
English intermediaries. Even in the last three love lyrics in
the Ker MS which directly contemplate death (and may
have been given their final placing for that reason), the link
is not made. Respectively they argue that faithfulness to
the beloved cancels fear of death; that death is a welcome
respite from pain and that, if a deity exists, earthly love

does not clarify his divine purpose. Cupid's vengeance is complete and the lover finds no refuge in the belief that love's pain may be a brief prelude to everlasting joy.

Montgomerie writes many fine lyrics in this tradition of late Petrarchism. Often he succeeds in maintaining the originality of approach earlier discussed and his heavy emphasis on topics such as Fortune's unfairness and the enmity of Time do suggest that, occasionally, literary convention is being employed to express personal obsessions.[14] There may even be covert references to particular affairs at Court, carefully disguised by the conventional mythological and imagistic apparatus of the tradition. But undeniably many of these poems come across as rhetorical exercises—clever but without substance—and those who see Montgomerie as a sort of tired postscript to the expertise of Dunbar and the energy of Alexander Scott usually draw their evidence from the 'Cupid' poems or the debate on freedom contained in MP XIII and XIV.

In so doing they ignore not only the more successful 'Petrarchan' poems but the many outstanding lyrics written in accordance with the broader Castalian attitude to love also expressed by James, Stewart of Baldynneis and others. Within that tradition, the 'maister poete' can indulge more fully his natural talents for argument, wit, invective and verbal inventiveness.

These poems first of all allow a more lighthearted and sensual approach than do the ones we have just been considering. When James chose a stanza to represent 'Materis of Love' in the *Reulis and Cautelis*, he spurned serious longings for an inaccessible lady, preferring to quote from Montgomerie's 'Before the Greeks durst enterpryse', a part song set to a lively rhythm in the harmonic style. In it the poet wittily compares the state of his current love affair with the position of the Greeks after consulting the oracle at Delphos. The mythological material is introduced just as subtly as in 'Echo' and the promise of complete victory over the Trojans is conveyed in lines which contain a sexual double-entendre. The message to poet/lover and to the Greeks is "To use them (her) hailly as they wold". And lest there be any doubt, the example is explicitly related to the poet's condition in the final stanza. If the Greeks rejoiced over the prophecy of victory in battle, how much more ecstatic should the poet be when contemplating capitulation of another kind:

> As evin the answer that I had
> Did gritly joy and comfort me,
> Quhen, lo! thus spak Apollo myne—
> All that thou seeks, it shall be thyne.
>
> (MP XXXVIII, 21–4)

Sex is a game and joyously the young Castalians celebrate it in song and verse.

If it is Stewart of Baldynneis who most favours lighthearted sensual wit of this sort, James's choice of the stanza shows that he also approved of it. In his *Amatoria* and *Reulis and Cautelis* the king urges another line completely at odds with the Petrarchan norm. Idealisation of the lady is rejected in the latter because it has become trite and in the former because it is an excess, opposed to his doctrine of the 'via media'. As a result his love sonnets to Anne promise to express a genuine affection but one between equal parties, each capable of human error. No other Renaissance writer known to me would dare to open a supposedly amorous sonnet to his beloved with the lines:

> O womans witt that wavers with the
>   winde
> When none so well may warie now as
>   I
> As weathercocke thy stablenes I
>   finde
> And as the sea that still can never lie[15]

curse

and end by excusing his lack of consistent ardour on the grounds that cares of state are preoccupying him.

Montgomerie, of course, is never as pedestrian or as blunt as this, but he and the other Castalians do compose lyrics demanding mutual admiration rather than one-sided service. 'ȝong tender plante! in spring tym of ȝour ȝeiris' is on one level a request, touchingly expressed, that his interests be valued as highly as hers:

> If I come speid, I think my tyme weill succeed
>   spent;
> And if I mis to mend it as I micht,
> I can reteir when resone thinks it richt.
> Thair is no match bot whair two
>   mutuall [meits]

(MP, 19–22)

Montgomerie uses a series of proverbs and the king's weathercock image to argue that his faithfulness is being poorly rewarded by fickleness and inconstancy. He openly espouses the 'live for the day' philosophy of Ronsard's 'Cueillez dés aujourd'huy les roses de la vie' and finally warns the lady that unless she gives him a straight reply, he will bestow his favours elsewhere. It is difficult to imagine a more unpetrarchan poem than this with its hectoring tone, insistence on equal rights and strong sexual undertones. Even the august figure of Fortune is reduced to the level of 'nevie nevie nak', a popular child's game, while a heavier use of Scots than is usual in his amorous verse reflects Montgomerie's down to earth approach.

Behind the work of all the Castalians there also lies a determination to merge particular experience of love with broader philosophical questions. James's rather un-fortunate desire to make the passion conform with his doctrine of moderation has already been mentioned. Stewart for his part has a series of sonnets and lyrics whose very titles—'Of Fidelitie', 'Of Chastitie', 'Of Truth'—convey this more serious, searching side to writing at the Scottish Court.

Montgomerie too could write love poetry in philosoph-

ical, even metaphysical vein without following the
Petrarchan line. Indeed two of his finest lyrics in different
ways relate his understanding of the passion to wider
questions. The first of these, 'Natur Passis Nuriture', takes
the form of a fable and develops the theme suggested by the
title with ironic subtlety. As in 'The Navigatioun' and *The
Flyting*, however, he never loses sight of his audience's
needs. Thus, in the opening stanza he addresses them
directly, breaks up the rhythm to convey the tones of
colloquial conversation, chooses simple language which
includes proverbs and familiar Scots words and establishes
a refrain which will throughout present the central thesis in
its most basic form:

> As Natur passis Nuriture,
>
> Of Natur all things hes a strynd;
>
> So everie leving creature
>
> Ay covets comounly thair kynd;
>
> As buks the dae—the harte the hynd—
>
> Lyk drawis to lyk, we sie this sure;
>
> So I am alwayis of that mynd,
>
> That Natur passis Nuriture.
>
> (MP XVIII, 1–8)

inclination

Having gained their attention, he vividly recounts the fate
of a hawk who spurned the attention of female birds of prey
in a spirit of pride. This theme, earlier treated in *The Buke
of the Howlat*, is developed through a series of ironies. The
result of his scorn is that it spreads to those who formerly
loved him, leaving him isolated. Then he falls not for a
creature higher than himself in Nature's order but for a
lowly kite. Remaining true to his vainglorious vision he
tries to make her worthy of him by feeding her food suited
to birds of prey but is cuckolded by an even lower bird, a
buzzard. Every one of these ironies reinforces the lesson of
the refrain. The more he tries to defeat Nature, the more
Nature revenges itself on him. Kites do not eat like hawks
nor do they remain true to one mate (a dual convention

elsewhere dramatised by Chaucer in *The Parlement of Foules*). Any attempt to set oneself apart from Nature's hierarchy will inevitably result in a humiliating reversal for the natural forces of the many will always prove too strong for a single rebel, however noble. It is therefore no accident that the hawk's fate is determined not only by the natural instincts of the kite and buzzard but broadcast to the world by the magpie obeying his natural love of gossip:

> Thair companie wes not quyet,
> But, or they wist, they wer bewryde,   betrayed
> And that throu pearking of a pyet.   impudence; magpie
>   (MP XVIII, 65–8)

Throughout Montgomerie writes with an effortless confidence, which tends to make you forget that he is using an interlacing rhymescheme and moving from light to heavy alliteration to mark out moments of high drama. The story not only provides a perfect and ironical illustration of the topic, the characters are vividly realised and dramatic asides maintain the audience's involvement throughout. Skilful variation of diction and rhythm also underline the bird's fate. Thus his early complacency is described in a stately measure and words shared with English:

> Thair wes a gentle girking gay,   hawk
> Of plesand plume and fair of flicht
>   (MP XVIII, 25–6)

But his ludicrous infatuation is depicted in colloquial Scots using heavy alliteration and a staccato beat:

> He grew so goked with that gled.   foolishly infatuated
>   (MP XVIII, 50)

In essence 'Natur passis Nuritur' counsels the lover against a passion which takes him beyond natural class barriers. It has therefore a serious message somewhat at odds with Petrarchism's code of obsessional aspiration.

'Ressave this harte', on the other hand, while raising even
more far-reaching metaphysical problems, has as its
central tenet the value of constancy to a single lady and this
the Italian poet would have approved. The poet's desire
for one kiss suggests that she, like Laura, has remained
chaste and the only essential difference lies in the fear that
he rather than the lady is about to die.

This lyric, which takes the form of a Testament, provides
a fitting conclusion to the examination of Montgomerie's
love lyrics for a variety of reasons. Here, some of the
Petrarchan conventions are observed—not only the
themes of fidelity and chastity but also the belief in stoical
patience. The metaphysical questions raised can also be
referred to the Petrarchan concern for life after death but
although the poet grants his spirit to God, he does not hope
for a purifying mystic love beyond the veil, dwelling rather
on the fact of human decay, which he describes with the
vivid physical detail of the Mediaeval death lyrics:

> That I am bot a carioun of clay,
>
> once   Quha quhylome lay about thy snawie
> throt.
>
> Now I must rot, wha some tym stoud so
>
> strong   stay.

(MP XXVII, 34–6)

In fact the poem looks forward tonally to Drummond of
Hawthornden's pessimistic reflections on mutability
rather than espousing the final spiritual optimism of
Petrarch's poems in Death. The first reason for grouping it
with the Castalian lyrics then is its independent consideration of the broader philosophical problems raised by
love.

It is, however, at the same time an intensely personal
poem. The lover recalls wistfully an afternoon in March,
when the lady had proved sympathetic to his grief. Then
he had prophesied his early death and that memory adds
poignancy to this later illness and to the will he is now

making. It is pointless to ask whether these particular
references refer to a real love. The point is that the poet
wishes to present his situation as if it were and to do this he
sets the work firmly within the framework of King James's
Court and another love and loyalty—the one he owes to
the king:

> My poesie I leave my prince to preiv;   evaluate
> No richt can reiv him of my rhetorie.
>
> (MP XXVII, 11–12)

This is the last major characteristic of the Castalian lyric,
occasional references to the circles round King James,
giving his love (whether real or imagined) an actual base in
place and time.

   In distinguishing these works from the Petrarchan lyrics
which outnumber them and by highlighting in turn their
wittiness, their less idealistic tone, their spirit of philosophical enquiry and their specific relationship to
one particular court, I am not making a sweeping literary judgment in their favour. Many of Montgomerie's
Petrarchan lyrics are among his best work. My res-
ervations are twofold. Sometimes the 'maister poete'
adopts Petrarchan ideas and images in a meekly imitative
manner. Any invention is lavished on the choice of verse
form or on perfecting a particularly extravagant rhetorical
trope. Such works would deservedly meet with the
approval of the court group for whom they were intended.
Even now we can appreciate the skills involved, but they
are essentially contributions to a courtly game, no more, no
less. Secondly, the idealism and the seriousness associated
with later Petrarchism deprived Montgomerie of some of
his most effective poetic weapons—the interplay of stylistic
levels, the sudden introduction of powerful invective,
couthy wit and the direct, simple tones of the plain man
speaking to plain men.

   'Ressave this harte' is written in Rime Batelée, adding a
caesura rhyme to his favourite interlacing pattern. It is

therefore every bit as demanding stylistically as any of the Petrarchan lyrics. It reaches moments of high dignity and expresses ideas just as altruistic as those inspired by Laura. But throughout there is a simplicity of expression, a directness of appeal which is Montgomerie's alone. And when contemplation of death leads him to sum up, he does not (as Burns did so often) mark this climax by raising the stylistic level and moving into a peroration in Latinate English. Rather he drops to the quiet tones of proverbial wisdom and the colloquialism of simple Scots:

> Thou wants the wight that never said
>   the nay:
> Adeu for ay! This is a lang guid nicht!
>
> (MP XXVII, 39–40)

In moments like this he proves himself a love lyricist of quality and originality, deserving critical recognition on his own terms and not through condescending comparisons with Dunbar or Alexander Scott.

iv

BIOGRAPHICAL LYRICS: In the ordering in the Ker MS the large group of love lyrics are preceded by six devotional poems. But between these two sections come five works dealing directly with Montgomerie's fall from courtly favour. They constitute one of the mini-sequences which characterise the manuscript and therefore their ordering as well as their quality seems to me significant.

Many of the technical skills noted in the analysis of the love lyric are also evident in this group. Montgomerie's mastery of a variety of verse forms, his ability to reinforce his message through intelligent use of classical myth and his frequent introduction of proverbs are all successfully diverted to this new purpose. But here he owes allegiance to no traditions and can speak out directly to his imagined audience, now wooing them with earnest advice as in 'The Navigatioun', now showing them that he retains the invective power which had characterised *The Flyting*. Heavy alliteration, forceful Scots words and continued rhetorical questioning are all brought into play as he outlines his griefs and identifies their cause. They may indeed all have been written during the time of his imprisonment as the last of the five suggests, but certainly they deal with that time when the poet longed for but did not receive support from king or Court.

They have been arranged according to three criteria. Their presentation of Montgomerie's complaints moves gradually from the general to the particular—from a discussion on Time which is based on personal experience but is advanced through proverbial wisdom to a detailed, embittered description of the poet's life in prison, deserted by all his supposed friends. Thematically, the first three lyrics emphasise in turn a different aspect of his fate—the power of Time; the deception practised towards him by the Court and his impotence against malicious Fortune. All these ideas—which also appear in his love lyrics—are taken up in the bitter tirade of the fourth and returned to more simply and stoically in the last. Tonally, we move from patient acceptance through increasing bitterness back to this determined stoicism, which has been made so much more impressive by our knowledge of the circumstances endured.

The opening work adopts the tones of an experienced, disillusioned teacher addressing an unspecified audience. His theme is contained in Montgomerie's favourite proverb "Tak tym in tym, or tym will not be tane", which also appears in his religious verse, in 'Ʒong, tender plante' and *The Cherrie and the Slae*. Here it introduces two stanzas of Ballat Royal and acts as the refrain. In the first verse the topic is developed through an allusion to the goddess Occasio, who was often associated with Fortune and was characterised by having hair only at the front of her head.

Just as despairing votaries could not grasp her as she
moved swiftly by, so Time sweeps on, leaving those who
are not swift enough to catch her bemoaning an irretriev-
able opportunity:

> Thou gettis no grippe agane fra sho be
>   gane.
>
> If thou wald speid, remember what I
>   spak—
>
> Take tyme in tyme or tym will not be
>   tane.

succeed

(MP I, 6–8)

The second stanza adds four new proverbs to the first one,
each reinforcing it and in particular stressing Time's destructive power and the folly of delay.

The vulnerability of the human condition has now been
established and the theme of Time thoroughly developed.
'The Oppositione of Court to Conscience', which follows,
maintains the tone of tired worldly wisdom but becomes
more particular in reference. The context is courtly, and
although Montgomerie does not yet name names, it is
clearly the Scottish Court which has given him the
experience from which he now sadly draws. The opening
line again proposes a thesis—"The Court and Conscience
wallis not weill". With slight variations it returns as the
refrain in each verse, so that even the most unwilling of
readers cannot escape the moral being taught.

This helps to unify the piece, but the major underlying
idea is that honesty and success at Court are irreconcil-
able. Only the deceiver will flourish, and with his usual
ingenuity Montgomerie uses a different method in each of
the five stanzas to illustrate the value of deception. The
theme is antithetically broached in the opening lines,
where loyalty is dismissed as an effective means of
advancement. Stanza 2 ironically suggests "honest adu-
lation" as a possible key and in stanza 3 Montgomerie uses
his knowledge of classical mythology vividly to satirise the

relationship between fawning courtier and praise-loving Prince: ·

> First thou mon preis thy Prince to pleis,   act energetically
> Thoght contrare Conscience he
>   commands,
> With Mercuris mouth and Argo's eis
> And with Briarius' hundreth hands;
> And seme whatsoevir he sayis to seill;
> So Court and Conscience wallis not   agree
>   weill.
>
> (MP II, 13–18)

Lying just below the surface here is the poet's earlier life; his composition of panegyrics on King James's early verse and, more generally, the fate of a Catholic who has had to compromise with his faith in order to be socially and politically acceptable.

The last two stanzas use respectively proverbial wisdom and direct indictment to give a complete and varied account of the crucial part played by deception in courtly advancement. Indeed in his final accusation Montgomerie introduces a Scots coinage 'glorifluikims' (servile expressions of flattery) to show how much he despises those who conform and flourish. While varying his approach so effectively, he also makes sure that every level is covered. You must deceive not only the powerful but your equals and servants too. This principle alone remains constant in a world where duplicity rules.

'Ane Invectione against Fortun' develops Montgomerie's case in a variety of ways. Most obviously it introduces the third theme—that of Fortune and the fall suffered by great men. Tonally, as we shall see, it covers a variety of moods but the reader senses a growing bitterness which must some time burst through. That bitterness, however, is directed against his enemies and while they are increasingly vilified, we, his privileged audience, are addressed more intimately than before as the poet becomes increasingly confidential.

By invoking Megaera, the Fate most closely associated with jealousy and ill will, Montgomerie economically acquaints us with his mood. His tale is a tragic one in the Mediaeval sense of a fall from heights to depths and it has inspired him with malevolent feelings against those forces which have caused it. Of these, Time is once more briefly mentioned but Fortune is the immediate object of his fury. In such a situation it is appropriate that he recalls the techniques which served him so well in *The Flyting*:

> Quhat epithets or arguments till use
>
> counterfeit   With fals and feinȝed Fortun for to flyte,
>
> Both wey my words and waill my verse
>   to wry[te,]
>
> Villain   That curst inconstant Cative till accuse,
>
> Quhais variance of all my wois I wyt.
>
> (MP III, 5–9)

Those very skills which gained him poetic eminence could now be used to attack those who have deprived him of it. And it is in flyting mood that the lyric opens with a series of graphic images emphasising Fortune's unreliability. But after 28 lines the approach alters and Montgomerie decides to express his bitterness in another way, by again drawing on that erudition so highly valued by the Castalians and their Maecenas in particular. His fate is as tragic as any described by Boccaccio in the *De Casibus Virorum Illustrium*:

> Thairin the fall of princes sall ȝe find.
>
> arrayed   That bloodie bitch, that buskit belly
>   blind
>
> forces; most valorous   Dings downwards ay the duchtiest lyk
>   Duiks,
>
> Quha hopped highest oft tyms comes
>   behind.
>
> (MP III, 42–5)

The bitterness is still evident and heavy alliteration aids invective but this change of focus heralds a more dramatic tonal alteration. From intense rancour against Fortune, the poet turns in confidential spirit to address us, "his friends". What has been a spirited personal battle now becomes a lesson which we should heed. Our case is not uniquely outwith Fortune's control for "Quhen ȝe leist wein, ȝour baks may to the wall". And to mark the new rational philosophical mood, Montgomerie ends with an exemplum, likening his state to that of Julius Caesar. Here his choice has been a careful one. The fate of Caesar, himself a writer, focuses attention on two aspects of Fortune which are particularly stressed in Montgomerie's verse. The first of these is the relationship between it and Time. If Caesar had read the proffered schedule at once, he would have lived. Instead he delayed and so fell victim to the knives of the conspirators. Secondly, the murder illustrates that Fortune may employ apparent friends just as often as enemies to overthrow you. In similar fashion Montgomerie had been betrayed by those he trusted.

In this poem the skills of the true 'makar' are again evident. The theme is briefly and clearly established at the outset. It is developed through the series of images and parallels, then by having recourse to authority in the shape of Boccaccio. It is brought home more closely to his readers in the conversational passage and related specifically to time and false friendship via the Caesar 'exemplum'. By careful variation of technique Montgomerie advances a controlled and effective 'Inventione' against Fortune, while touching lightly on the earlier themes of Time and Deception. But he does this within the ostensibly altruistic context of providing friendly advice for the benefit of those who have not yet fallen.

In many ways the next lyric 'The Poet's Complaint at his Nativity' sounds as if it is meant to be a final comment. Tonally it reaches new heights of ferocity. Now we definitely are in the realms of flyting, with no fewer than twenty-eight impassioned questions being hurled at Fortune, the Court and the king, as the furious poet tries desperately to account for his fall.

Thematically it translates the themes of Time, deception and Fortune into cosmic terms. Why, Montgomerie asks, did all the astrological signs at his birth appear so benevolent if their only purpose was to exacerbate a tragic life? In apportioning blame, he gives us the most searching account of Fortune so far. He relates its powers on the one hand to the Pagan Gods and on the other to the Muses, using Apollo as linking figure. In mythological terms such an interrelationship was well established. As Seznec notes:

> The eminent place given to Apollo ... has a dual explanation. Not only does he conduct the choir of the Muses, who set in motion the planets ... but he himself has his abode in the midst of the Planets like the Dorian mode amid the strings of the lyre ... He is thus both the origin and the centre of the Universal Harmony.[16]

This conventional scenario permits Montgomerie to link the misery he has suffered generally (the planets) with the specific misfortunes endured as an artist (the muses). But it is the emphasis on Apollo which gives this poem its personal venom. Throughout the sequence the guilt of James VI has been kept in the background. Now, in the guise of Apollo (a rôle earlier assigned to him by Montgomerie in his panegyrical sonnets) he reappears as the ruler-artist who first encouraged, then rejected the poet:

> Quhy did Apollo Poet me proclame,
> To cleith my heid with his grene laurell
>   cap,
> Since that the Hevins ar hinderers of my
>   hap?   (MP IV, 33–5)

A particular reference to James in line 41 makes all this explicit but no reader aware of Montgomerie's history

could fail to have made the equation earlier. Nor are we (or
the king) allowed the comforting illusion that perhaps the
poet has adopted a dramatic rôle and (in James's own
words) "sung of sorrows never felt by me".[17] In stanza 5
there appears the line

> EXTOLD AMONG YE RARE MEN
> wes my name.
>
> (MP IV, 32)

The capitalisation in the MS gives the hint. That name in
anagrammatic form is Alexander Montgomerye.

If this lyric gives an overall view of Montgomerie's tragic
fortune as man and poet, while bitterly identifying James
as the ultimate cause, it also poses questions of deeper
theological significance:

> Quhy wes my birth on Eister day at morne?
>
> (MP IV, 17)

> Quhy wes my will to vertue mair then
> vyce?
>
> (MP IV, 43)

The poet was born on Easter Sunday, the day of Christ's
resurrection, and has been a virtuous man throughout his
life. This appeal to morality and the Christian story draws
him towards an even darker conclusion. In Renaissance
mythology the planetary Gods were subject to the
Christian God. In the Renaissance theory of history, the
king was likewise God's vassal. Why, Montgomerie's long
series of questions demands, does that divine power allow
so much injustice to be suffered by the talented and the
virtuous? No positive answer is offered; only the plaintive
conclusion that the way of truth may be the way of folly:

> Forgive me this, and if I do it agane
> Then tak me with the foxis taill[18] a flap,
> Since that the Hevins are hinderers of
> my hap.
>
> (MP IV, 47–9)

After the stridency and the high seriousness of 'The Poet's Complaint', the quieter tones of 'No wonder thoght I waill and weip' may come as something of an anti-climax. But it is placed last for a number of obvious reasons. It culminates the movement towards increasing intimacy by revealing the poet's actual feelings in the prison from where the whole sequence may have been written. Simply and without affectation it describes his loneliness and his attempts to disguise his grief for the benefit of visitors. As readers we are invited to come closer to him than ever before. Like 'The Poet's Complaint' it draws together the three major themes, but expresses them with a detachment and simplicity which suggests victory over the destructive powers of bitterness. One must not trust appearances for

glitters   All is not gold that gleitis;

               (MP V, 42)

man is almost always out of step with Time and nature:

an unappointed time For man may meit at unsetstevin
       Thoght montanis nevir meits;

             (MP V, 47–8)

the poet has fallen from glory but cannot expel memories of the past:

   Remembring me whair I haif bene
   Both lykit and belovt.

             (MP V, 33–4)

Finally it returns to the tones of world-weary but kindly counsel which make the horror of his experience at once a bond with and a lesson for the sympathetic reader:

   Then do as ȝee wald be done to
   Belovit brethren all;
   For out of doubt, quhat so ȝe do,
   Resaiv the lyk ȝe sall.

             (MP V, 49–52)

Only in the biographical sonnets will Montgomerie again reveal his own problems in such a moving and direct way.

v

RELIGIOUS LYRICS: Before looking in some detail at the Religious Lyrics in the Ker MS, it is necessary to note the appearance in 1605 of a volume entitled *The Mindes Melodie*. It contains fifteen psalms, a 'Song of Simeon' and a 'Gloria Patri', all written in the complex eighteen-line stanza used by Montgomerie for 'The Solsequium', and set to its tune. No author is named but there can be no doubt that two psalms at least (Nos 1 and 23) are by the 'maister poete' because they have appeared earlier in the Ker and Bannatyne MSS respectively. Any minor variations between the versions involve the sort of anglicisation commonly practised by printers when setting Scots texts at this time.

Despite the fact that the sustained quality of these fifteen songs, uniting simple diction effortlessly to complex metre, forces us to assume another writer of Montgomerie's class and using Montgomerie's methods if we are to deny him the collection as a whole, that is the position I should have taken in the absence of further evidence. After all, his name is nowhere mentioned and the composition of psalms in the vernacular is an activity more usually associated with Protestants than Catholics. As P. M. Smith notes in his book on Marot, "the translation of Psalms into French (was) a task to which Calvin had attached the utmost importance since the time of his installation in Geneva in 1537".[19] Knox and the Church of Scotland shared this enthusiasm and it might have been presumed that a poet with strong Catholic leanings would have kept himself apart from plans aimed at improving the Protestant mode of service.

Yet that is precisely what Montgomerie did not do.

When, in 1631, the Kirk set its face against the new edition
of Psalms translated mainly by William Alexander but
advertised as being King James's own, one of the major
objections advanced was that the General Assembly had
not been consulted. On this ground the approach of an
earlier poet was held up as a contrasting model. That poet
was Montgomerie, who had presented his psalms modestly
and through the proper channels:

> Alexr Montgomerie had a singular vaine of poesie, ȝit
> he tuik a more modest course, for he translated bot a
> few for a proofe, and offered his travells in that kynde
> to the kirk.[20]

It therefore seems likely that *The Mindes Melodie*
preserves Montgomerie's offerings. They may even, as Mrs
Shire suggests, have been intended "to commemorate the
death of the poet in mourning ceremony",[21] although the
gap of seven years and the failure to name him at any point
in the publication leave room for doubt. What is most
interesting is that Montgomerie did not allow religious
principles to prevent him placing his talents politely at the
service of the Kirk.

The eight religious lyrics which appear in the Ker MS
have, as before noted, been given a position of extreme
importance. Six of them open the collection, preceding the
major groups of biographical lyrics, love lyrics and sonnets.
And if the secular works concentrate on human mis-
fortune, injustice and mutability, these six poems by way of
contrast stress divine benevolence, mercy and eternal life.
This consolatory perspective begins with Montgomerie's
versions of the first and second psalms, each promising final
victory to the good man and destruction to his evil
counterpart. The first concentrates on the positive,
virtuous side of the equation, the second on the negative,
evil side but both celebrate a salvation and judgement
beyond this world. Once these have established that
salvation does exist, 'The Poet's Dreme' uses parable,

proverb and mystic vision to argue that it can be attained by the persevering Christian. 'A Godly Prayer' next voices an intensely personal penitential plea, establishing the correct and false attitudes possible to the new law of Mercy instituted by Christ, while 'A Walkning from Sin' urges immediate repentance and adherence to the three theological virtues as sure passports for even the worst of sinners. The opening group is rounded off by 'A Leson how to Leirne to Die' which, as its title suggests, is influenced by the 'Ars Moriendi' tradition. Man will finally be deserted by all the gifts God has lent him but will carry his penance and "good deeds" on to a divine Justice which "haldis the ballance evin" and a death which opens the door to everlasting life.

If these poems discuss the problems and pitfalls facing the Christian pilgrim, the last two sound out a note of triumph in contemplating the divine love offered to those who reject the world and become brides of the Lamb:

> 3ea, Chryst, these earthly toyes
> Sall turne in hevinly joyes.
> Let the world be gone:,
> I'l love CHRYST allone.
>
> (DP VII, 35–8)

> Now thou hes that thou desyrit—
> Me to be thy Lord and Love—
> All the things that thou requyrit,
> To the heir, I do approve.
>
> (DP VIII, 41–4)

It may be that DP VIII ('Come my Childrene') with its heavy reliance on *The Song of Songs* and reference to marriage with God may be specifically related to Montgomerie's priestly aspirations but this does not seem to me certain. Nor am I, like Cranstoun, greatly concerned as to whether these powerful expressions of religious triumph were occasionally glimpsed amid miseries or represent the final judgement of maturity.[22] It is enough

that whoever ordered the Ker MS chose to end a collection
dominated by worldly defeats on an uncompromising note
of spiritual optimism.

Detailed analysis of the lyrics reveals that, although this
consolation would commend itself to all Christians, they
are clearly written from a Catholic viewpoint. Most
notably in 'The Poet's Dreme' he stresses that only those
who unite faith to good works may enter the Kingdom of
Heaven:

> 3it he hes said that sik men sall
> Whais faith brings furth gude frute.

(DP III, 11–12)

Based on St James 2.17, this was the accepted Catholic
position. It was opposed by both Luther and Calvin who
argued that in the Gospel there was only one work, the
internal work of faith whose action could not be other than
good:

> Thus it cannot be that faith in him is otiose, but it lives
> and works and triumphs and thus its works flow
> spontaneously outward from faith.[23]

Montgomerie on more than one occasion in his devotional
verse stresses merit and consistently upholds the possibility
that faith may be unfulfilled in action.

It is not only in specific points of doctrine that his
Catholicism is revealed. He adheres to the more general
traditions of Catholic thought. 'A Leson how to Leirne to
Die' relies heavily on ideas advanced in mediaeval works
such as *The Book of the Craft of Dying* and *The Mirrour of St
Edmunde*. The sinner is guided to a holy death, first by
coming to know himself:

> Exame 3our selfis; se what 3e ar,

(DP VI, 3)

just as the reader of *The Mirrour* is counselled "to þe
knaweyng of þi selfe may þou com with besy umbythynk-

ynge". Death appears suddenly, demanding that the books
of life be presented in preparation for the Day of Judgment,
when the gifts of Fortune and Nature ("beutie, riches, wit
and strenth") will fade away, leaving only good deeds
("prayers, almesdeids") to speak for the penitent. The
pattern is very close to that presented in the Morality
Drama *Everyman* and both works rely on ideas and imagery
cultivated by the 'Ars Moriendi' tradition.

Echoes of the Catholic liturgy are also prevalent,
especially in the penitential poems. When Montgomerie
writes in 'A Godly Prayer'

3it damne me noght whom thou hes
    boght so deir
Sed salvum me fac, dulcis Fili Dei,   But make me safe, o gentle Son of God
                    (DP IV, 13–14)

a practising Catholic would associate the Latin words with
the Response after the ninth Lesson of the Dead and so
have an enriched sense of the finality of earthly life and the
terrors of damnation being stressed by the poet. In general,
however, Montgomerie draws his material from a wide
knowledge of Scripture. New Testament echoes are
skilfully inserted into Old Testament tales; Old Testament
maxims mingle with Christ's teachings as the poet subtly
counterpoints the ages of justice and mercy.

That is, although the devotional poems are clearly the
work of a devout Catholic, they do not breathe a
combative, missionary spirit. Essentially personal, they
consistently choose the Catholic means to salvation rather
than the Protestant but they do not emphasise major
doctrinal conflicts in a belligerent manner. Personal
consolation founded on basic Catholic teaching rather
than direct conflict with opposing creeds seems to be
Montgomerie's aim.

All the religious lyrics make powerful emotional appeals
and they do so while maintaining that verbal simplicity
which the spokesman for the General Assembly had found

lacking in the James VI/William Alexander collection.
The two psalms in the Ker MS like those in *The Mindes
Melodie* carefully avoid "French, Latine, and hard
Englisch tearmes"[24] and are set to popular secular tunes, so
that they may be understood by the common people. The
opening stanza of Psalm 1 demonstrates the ease with
which Montgomerie masters the demanding 'Solsequium'
stanza while maintaining the original imagery and using
only the simplest of words:

> Weill is the man,
> ʒea blessed than,
> Be grace that can
> Esheu ill counsell and the godles gait;
> That stands not in
> The way of sin
> Nor does begin
> To sitt with mockers in the scornefull
>   sait;
> Bot in Jehovah's law
> Delyts aricht
> And studies it to knaw
> Both day and nicht;
> For he sall be
> Lyk to the trie
> Quhilk plantit by the running river
>   growis;
> Quhilk frute does beir
> In tym of ʒeir;
> Quhais leaf sall never fade nor rute sall
>   louis.

loosen

(DP I, 1–18)

If he could have set all the Psalms in this ambitious stanza
form he would have proved yet again his versatility as a
'makar' and one cannot repress the futile regret that his
offer was not accepted and lesser men and metres were
finally preferred.

Equally impressive is the unobtrusive way in which he uses his extensive scriptural knowledge to convey his message. Surprisingly, there is evidence of this even in the Psalms, which are usually regarded as strict translations. In Psalm 2, for example, when God rejoices in having set up his king on Mount Sion, Montgomerie's version reads:

> I will declair his will thairfoir;
> That is, that he
> Hes said to me,
> "Thou art my Sone beloved ay,
> From whome my Love
> Sall not remove;
> I haif begotten thee this day."

(DP II, 16–22)

The word "beloved" and the two succeeding lines have, of course, no equivalent in the Vulgate. Subtly Montgomerie has introduced the typological link between David and Christ by drawing in material from Matthew 3.17 and the Christmas Vespers. It is an important addition for it gives a new context to the view of Salvation, setting new law beside old.

Foreseeably he uses these techniques with greater freedom in his original lyrics. Considerations of space dictate that I illustrate this point by looking at one poem— 'The Poet's Dreme'—in depth but he uses the same methods with equal success in almost all the others. 'The Dreme' opens with a brief account of the parable of the wise and foolish virgins. The diction is simple and the poet's desire for salvation clearly stated in a colloquial tone strengthened by the use of the Scots word 'wedfie' (reward). He does not, however, mention the equal numbers of virgins on each side, suggesting that half the petitioners gain eternal life. Instead, in the next stanza he presents his readers with the much more pessimistic view of *Matthew* 7.14:

> The way is strait, the nomber small,
> Therefore we may not entir all.
>
> (DP III, 9–10)

The difficulty of the quest is highlighted and when he does
return to the original parable, it is to dramatise more
vividly the shutting of the door and to urge the value of
perseverance, an idea common in his own secular verse but
not present in the original version:

> My [spreit] then, fash not for a fall,
> Contineu knocking, clim and call.
> Thair is no winning ouer the wall
> Fra ains the dur be shute.
>
> (DP III, 13–16)

The Biblical story is manipulated so that it fits in more
exactly with the poet's vision. It therefore comes as no
surprise when the moral drawn by Christ, "Watch
therefore, for ye know neither the day nor the hour when
the Son of man cometh", is replaced by one of
Montgomerie's favourite proverbs:

> Tak tym in tyme or tym be tint.
>
> (DP III, 17)

Indeed the whole of the third stanza is taken up with
proverbial wisdom and only in the fourth do we return to
a specific passage in Scripture, with the vision of Jacob.
Montgomerie isolates that part of the tale which sees the
ladder as a means of ascent into Heaven but he also adds
from *Exodus* the idea of the sacred name and from *John* (or
Revelation) the idea of Christ as Lamb of God:

> Assure they self, it is the sam
> Wharby the godly fathers clam,
> Wha war the heires of Abraham,
>   Beloved of the Lord.
> If thou beleive into that Lamb
> Who said, "I am evin that I am,"
> The De'ill dou nevir the condam;
> Thy warand is the word.
>
> (DP III, 33–40)

As in Psalm 2 he uses typology to link Old Testament and New, so making a smooth transition to the final stanza with its identification of Christ's sacrifice as the new ladder:

> Then clim by Chryst for, I conclude,
> Thy help lyes in his hands.
>
> (DP III, 47–8)

The message of 'The Poet's Dreme' is at once traditional and personal. This is Montgomerie's own dream, translating into spiritual terms those concerns about time, perseverance and love which dominate his secular writing. And as always the material has been carefully arranged to make the most powerful impact possible. Old Testament material links with New; parable gives way to proverbs, to vision and finally to the reassuring echoes of the Liturgy. Scriptural material is reshaped so that the poet's concerns may be highlighted and imaginative unity maintained.

Cranstoun does not recognise the Montgomerie of the religious verse. "Never was transformation more complete. With him life's pantomime is past. We have now no longer any of the quaint and pithy proverbs that danced in a maze of many-twinkling feet in 'The Cherrie and the Slae'; nothing of the wild rollicking verse of 'The Flyting'; ... nothing of the ecstatic joy or of the many-voiced notes that chimed in varying numbers in the Miscellaneous Poems" (i.e. the secular lyrics).[25] I recognise him only too well. The proverbs have not disappeared, only changed their context; the flyting techniques are no less powerful because they focus on the Devil ("in stinking sty with Satans sinfull swyn") rather than Polwart; the many voices and varying numbers are just as evident; and those brief moments of amorous ecstasy occasionally voiced in the love poems achieve a sustained fulfilment in spiritual love given and received. As for Montgomerie's attitude to life's pantomime (waiving the unsuitability of the metaphor for his case), the religious lyrics do not bypass his concerns with fortune, time and death but transcend them by placing behind the first a beneficent creator, around the second eternity and above the third Christ's cross. It is the focus, not the man nor the poet, which has changed.

NOTES

1. Other minor sources include the *Bannatyne MS*, the *Maitland Quarto MS*, *The Mindes Melodie* and Laing MS III, 447. Stevenson prints a number of lyrics from the last of these but very few can with confidence be assigned to Montgomerie.
2. I am grateful to Professor John MacQueen for pointing this out to me.
3. *Poems of James*, *op. cit.*, II, 107.
4. *Maitland Folio MS*, p. 32.
5. See, for example, MP XXVIII, 'Melancholie, grit deput of Dispair'.
6. Lois Borland, "Montgomerie and the French Poets of the Early Sixteenth Century", *Modern Philology*, XI, 1913–14, pp. 127–34.
7. P. H. Smith, *Clément Marot*, London, 1970, p. 81.
8. *Clément Marot: Les Epigrammes*, ed. C. A. Mayer, London, 1970, p. 149.
9. *Poems of James*, *op. cit.*, I, 79.
10. K. Elliott, *Music of Scotland 1500–1700*, 2 vols., Cambridge dissertation, 1954. (Volume I unpublished; volume II published as Elliott and Shire, *Music of Scotland 1500–1700*, Musica Britannica, XV, 2nd Edition, London, 1964.)
11. Shire, *Song, Dance and Poetry*, *op. cit.*, pp. 139–80.
12. Elliott, *op. cit.*, I, 122.
13. *Poems of James*, *op. cit.*, I, 77.
14. R. D. S. Jack, "The Theme of Fortune in the Verse of Alexander Montgomerie", *Scottish Literary Journal*, X, 1983, pp. 25–44.
15. *Poems of James*, *op. cit.*, II, 72.
16. Jean Seznec, *The Survival of the Pagan Gods*, London, 1940, p. 142.
17. *Poems of James*, *op. cit.*, II, 78.
18. The fox's tail was one of the badges of a jester.
19. Smith, *op. cit.*, p. 35.
20. *The Bannatyne Miscellany*, Bannatyne Club, 3 vols., Edinburgh, 1827, I, 237.
21. Shire, *Song, Dance and Poetry*, *op. cit.*, p. 116.
22. Cranstoun, *op. cit.*, p. xxxix.
23. Luther's Works 57.113.21. as translated by Gordon Rupp, *The Righteousness of God*, London, 1953, p. 205.
24. *The Bannatyne Miscellany*, *op. cit.*, I, 240.
25. Cranstoun, *op. cit.*, p. xxxviii.

CHAPTER IV

THE SONNET

All those sonnets which can definitely be ascribed to Montgomerie are to be found in the Ker MS. A group of seventy follow 'A Cartell', preceding only the final two Devotional Poems, 'Away! vane warld' and 'Come my childrene dere, draw neir me'. Of the seventy, three (Nos 30, 66 and 68) are not by the poet, the first being attributed to Christen Lyndesay and the other two to Montgomerie's friend Hugh Barclay of Ladyland.[1] But elsewhere in the collection there appear two epitaphs, to Sir Robert Drummond of Carnok and the Shaw brothers, which adopt the form. To these sixty-nine sonnets it is tempting to add some of the poems edited by Stevenson from Laing MS. III, 447.[2] On grounds of quality and style, I should be inclined to credit him at least with 'I dreamit ane dreame, o that my dreame wer trew' and 'First serve, syne sute, quhiles seme to lichlie luif'. But there is no signature and therefore no certainty.

It is even more tempting to follow Cranstoun and give him one of the two earliest known Scottish sonnets in the Bannatyne MS. '3e, Inglische hursone! sumtyme will avant' immediately precedes the lyric replying to 'Ane Helandmanis Invective', which definitely is Montgomerie's. It displays the sort of ingenious wordplay which characterises many of his sonnets.[3] But again his name does not appear. Clear attributions are made for six other Montgomerie poems in the MS and so, on balance, the evidence seems to warn us against adding this poem to the canon.

Before looking at the Ker sonnets in detail, it is

important to place the Scottish sonnet in a wider context
and, in particular, to identify those features which distinguish it from sonnet writing in England and Europe.
Chronologically, for example, it is a late movement, only
becoming popular in the early 1580s when it was
enthusiastically adopted by the Castalians. True, the
presence in the Bannatyne MS of '3e, Inglische hursone!'
and 'Lyk as the littill Emmet haith hir gall' proves that the
form was used prior to 1568. But the major sonneteers—
Montgomerie, James VI, William Fowler and John
Stewart—only began to use it regularly after the 'band'
had been formally established. It was given the royal seal of
approval in 1584 when the king introduced his *Essayes of
a Prentise* with twelve sonnets imploring the Pagan Gods
to aid him in his work. Prominent Castalians, including
Montgomerie, contributed dedicatory sonnets, while the
king added two further examples to introduce the section
containing *The Reulis and Cautelis*.

If it took longer to gain popularity in Scotland than
England, so it maintained that popularity longer. R. H.
MacDonald has correctly noted that nearly all the major
English sonnet sequences had been composed before 1597.[4]
Most of the major Scottish sequences—Sir William
Alexander's *Aurora*, Alexander Craig's *Amorose Songes,
Sonets and Elegies* as well as Drummond's *Poems* and *Flowres
of Sion*—were written after the Union of the Crowns, with
the last of them being published as late as 1630.

The word sequence suggests a second distinguishing
feature. We do normally think of sonnet sequences and
associate the form with love. These assumptions hold for
Scottish sonnet composition in the seventeenth century.
But of the early Castalians only William Fowler produces
a love sequence of any length (*The Tarantula of Love*).
Montgomerie, as we shall see, prefers much shorter groups,
none of which contain more than five poems, while, of the
sixty-nine sonnets generally agreed to be his, only twenty-
seven at most could be said to deal with love. Of these

many are commissioned poems dealing with the lives and
marriages of courtiers. As such they might more accurately
be classed as Occasional verse. Only nine of Stewart's
sonnets deal with the passion and (if the formal, erudite
Amatoria can really be accepted as justifying its title)
thirteen of James's fifty-eight. For what then was the
sonnet form primarily used?

The king in *The Reulis and Cautelis* gives a brief answer:

> For compendious praysing of any bukes, or the
> authouris thairof, or ony argumentis of uther his-
> toreis, quhair sindrie sentences, and change of
> purposis are requyrit.[5]

The sonnet is not linked with love. It is suited for eulogies
and for topics involving the presentation of different
viewpoints or twists in argument. The king is here
describing early Castalian practice and giving his support
to the broader thematic range granted to the form at court.
For the Castalians the sonnet could be used for courtly
compliment, for moral or theological argument or for
personal petitions. The "change of purposis" might be
contained within a single sonnet, making use of the
octet/sestet or quatrain/couplet division, or it could be
advanced in short groups of sonnets with the fourteen-line
form becoming part of a larger unit. Personal expressions
of love were not shunned but the court poet would also use
the sonnet to celebrate the love of others in epithalamion or
panegyric. The difference between Castalian practice and
that elsewhere is, of course, not absolute. Italian, French
and English sonneteers did occasionally use the form for
these varied purposes. It is one of emphasis and only in
Scotland before 1603 does love cease to dominate and the
potential of the sonnet for eulogy and argument become so
fully developed.

A third feature which distinguishes the Scottish sonnet
from the English in particular relates to source preferences.
As the earlier discussion of the lyric has demonstrated,

Scottish writers preferred to imitate French rather than Italian models. The same preference emerges for the sonnet for reasons I have fully analysed elsewhere.[6] Again William Fowler proves an exception, drawing primarily on Petrarch and the Petrarchists when compiling *The Tarantula*. But James in his sonnets imitates Desportes and Saint Gelais, while the former is also the strongest single influence on John Stewart. Montgomerie for his part turns to Ronsard. As Oscar Hoffman first pointed out, seven of his sonnets derive from Ronsardian originals.[7] In some instances the relationship is not very close. Only rhetorical similarities and close echoing of the final line betrays the debt of 'Bright amorous ee whare Love in ambush [lyes]' to 'Oeil, qui portrait dedans les miens reposes'. On the other hand the variations between 'Heureuse fut l'estoille fortunée' and 'O happy star at evning and at morne' are for the most part those rendered inevitable by the task of translating from one language into another. Between these extremes we have close imitation of the octet only ('Pardonne moy, Platon, si je ne cuide'/'Excuse me Plato if I suld suppone') and condensation of twenty lines into fourteen ('Hyer au soir que je pris maugré toy'/'So swete a kis ȝistrene fra thee I reft'). The precise technique, therefore, varies but the frequency with which Montgomerie returns to his favourite source suggests genuine admiration. This is particularly so as King James was known to prefer the more spiritual vision of Du Bartas and to mistrust Ronsard's views on kingship and enthusiasm for Mary.

This reliance on French sources was part of the Castalian desire to emphasise the difference between their practice and that of England. This is not to deny the frequent visits to Edinburgh and Stirling of poets from south of the border but direct influence can be overstressed. Brotanek's claims for influence from Wyatt are generally not convincing.[8] 'Thyne ee the glasse whare I beheld my hairt' is simply a re-writing in Scots of a sonnet by Constable, and although 'Against the God of Love' may well have been inspired by Sonnet 98 in Watson's *Hekatompathia* it is only the general idea of a flyting against Cupid which Montgomerie may have taken from the English writer; particular echoes are non-existent. After 1603 most Scottish poets would seek a cultural as well as a political union but the Castalians strove to maintain a separate identity. The preference for French sources was part of this effort.

The fourth major distinguishing feature is formal. Both of the Bannatyne sonnets adopt interlacing rhymeschemes. The one followed in '3e, Inglische hursone!'—ABABBCBCCDCDEE—is usually thought to originate with Spenser but had been adopted in Scotland well before the *Amoretti*. In *The Essayes of a Prentise* all of James's sonnets use it and the five sonnets of dedication follow suit. Although Montgomerie had probably employed this scheme before 1584, the king's example established it as the norm in Scottish sonneteering. He goes on to use it for fifty out of his fifty-eight sonnets, while it accounts for thirty-two of Stewart's thirty-three and a hundred and eight of Fowler's hundred and twenty-nine. Montgomerie experiments more widely and uses seven different rhymeschemes, mostly based on an ABBAABBA octet, but he too is a Castalian and thirty-nine of his sixty-nine sonnets adopt the interlacing pattern. Its origins may again lie with the grands rhétoriqueurs but perhaps in this instance we need not seek so far. In the sixteenth-century Scottish lyric the eight-line Ballat Royal with its ABABBCBC scheme is by far the most popular stanza. Using this as the octet, it would be easy to derive the 'Spenserean' scheme from native practice. Whether this be the case or not, Castalian preference for the interlacing form was marked. After the Union, William Alexander and David Murray used it sparingly but at the Edinburgh court there was a real sense in which adoption of that particular rhyme pattern proved membership of the band.

Mrs Shire suggests a further distinguishing characteristic between Scottish and English sonneteering when she
claims that some sonneteers at the Scottish court, notably
Thomas Hudson and Montgomerie, wrote sonnets with
musical settings in mind.[9] Certainly the former, who was a
musician, did regard one complimentary sonnet as a part-
song but for the basis of the argument as it applies to
Montgomerie we have to return to the Ronsardian
adaptations. Earlier critics, Mrs Shire correctly argues,
were wrong to compare these Scots sonnets with the later
1584 printings of the *Amours*. After all, 'O happy star' was
composed in 1582 and a study of the French variants
proves that Montgomerie did not use either that text or the
earlier edition of 1578 for his other Ronsardian sonnets. On
the other hand, Mrs Shire's claim that "It was not as a
sequence but as a book of sonnet part-songs that *Les Amours*
made its impact on Montgomerie"[10] rests on her belief that
he used the first 1552 edition with its musical supplement.
The first trouble here is that only four of the seven
Ronsardian sonnets appeared in that text. All seven
appear in the *Oeuvres* of 1560 and 1567. Moreover, in cases
where the 1552 text differs from these editions, Montgomerie follows the latter. Thus, in 'Excuse me Plato' the
line

vaulted   That underneth the hevinly vauted
                            round

(S LVI, 2)

follows the version first printed in 1560

Que sous le rond de la voute des Dieus

rather than that of 1552

Que soubz la vouste et grande arche des
      dieux.

Likewise in 'Bright amorous ee' the line

Cleir cristal tear distilde at our depairt

(S XXXIX, 2)

is closer to the 1560 and 1567 versions, which specify a tear "d'argent", than that of 1552, which does not.

Neither the 1560 nor the 1567 edition contained music. They were also texts possessed by James VI and would have been available for the 'maister poete' to consult. From either Montgomerie could have got all the texts necessary for his adaptations. These are usually closer to his Scots versions than either the 1552 poems or those later editions with "musical associations" which Mrs Shire uses for those sonnets not available at the earlier date. Thus she suggests that 'So swete a kis ȝistrene' is based on the thirty-four-line 'Harsoir Marie'. But the first line in the 1560 text, like Montgomerie's version, makes no mention of Marie, reading simply "Hyer au soir que je pris maugré toy". It is also much shorter, a twenty-line piece which Montgomerie follows closely for the first twelve lines, merely condensing the last eight into a couplet.

It is of course possible that Montgomerie had heard that some of Ronsard's sonnets had been set to music, even although he did not follow the 1552 text. As no musical settings for any of his sonnets have survived, however, that must remain a hypothesis. And, ironically, when he refers to the muses 'singing' his sonnets at Cupid's court he may well not be writing literally but following Ronsard's example in another way—using musical ideas in the context of classical mythology "to construct a highly extended metaphor for the writing of poetry".[11] There may indeed have been a closer relationship between music and the sonnet form in Scotland than in England but the case does not seem to me fully proved.

The traditions of Scottish sonneteering just outlined were of course largely created by Montgomerie as 'maister poete' and therefore it comes as no surprise to find the sonnets in the Ker MS covering a wide variety of themes and exhibiting many different styles. Passionate expressions of love mingle with arguments on moral and theological issues; personal complaints over his pension follow eulogies on courtiers or on the king's qualities as a poet; dignified pleas that scurrilous verses have wrongfully been attributed to him precede lighter works celebrating the joys of friendship and drink. It is the range which first impresses, the effortless movement from dignified praise in the high style to couthy colloquialism or scurrilous invective in flyting mode.

But, as with the lyrics, the arrangement of the poems is not entirely haphazard. Again, the series opens and closes with poems which proclaim higher spiritual values thus enclosing the more worldly verse which numerically dominates. The very first sonnet is a powerful hymn to the Trinity, using oxymoron and triple groupings stylistically to underline the mystery and paradox of a Godhead, three in one:

> Unmov't wha movis Thee round about
>   the Ball,
> Contener unconteind, is, was and sall

enduringly constant

> Be sempiternall, mercifull and just.
> Creator uncreatit, now I call.
> Teich me Thy treuth since into Thee I
>   trust.
> Incres, confirme and strenthen from
>   above

but more than the rest

> My faith, my hope bot by the lave my
>   Love.   (S I, 8–14)

It is followed by an exploration of the divine purpose as revealed by the wonders of the universe which transmits the poet's awe through compound words.

vaulted

> High architectur, wondrous-vautit-
>   rounds;
> Huge-host of Hevin in restles-rolling
>   spheers;

axletree (axis)

> Firme-fixt polis whilk all the axtrie
>   beirs;
> Concordant-discords, swete harmonious
>   sounds.   (S II, 1–4)

Once more we are conscious of the makar decorously suiting diction to theme, this time suggesting that the normal limits of vocabulary are inadequate to convey the perfection of the supernatural scheme.

But if God is perfect, man is not and three sonnets in the opening group make appeals against vice addressed directly to God (S III), to the preacher Patrick Galloway (S VI) and to the king (S VII). In these Montgomerie displays his own skills in pulpit rhetoric while commenting on events of the day. But if his theology is becoming increasingly practical and particular, he still argues, in different mode, for the victory of spiritual values over worldliness. And it is this theme which is picked up in (S LXX), the final sonnet of the whole series. 'Against the God of Love' may be a flyting and stand in marked stylistic contrast to the earlier praising of Trinity and universe, but in attacking the embodiment of earthly desire, the poet speaks out just as forcefully for spiritual truth in the low style as earlier he had in the high:

Art thou a god? No—bot a gok disguysit;	fool
A bluiter buskit lyk a Belly blind	scoundrel; arrayed; fiend
With wings and quaver waving with the wind;	quiver
A plane playmear for vanitie devysit.	playfellow
Thou art a stirk for all thy staitly stylis	idiot
And these good geese whom sik a god begylis.	such

(S LXX, 9–14)

A series which opens by praising the God of true love thus ends by rejecting the God of false love, an arrangement which also leads naturally into the triumphant assertions of 'Away! vane world' and 'Come, my Children dere', which follow in the manuscript.

The fact that the overall ordering of the sonnets in this way mirrors that of the sequence as a whole strengthens the theory that the Ker MS has been designed to present

Montgomerie's work in a way which emphasises spiritual concerns. The responsibility for this arrangement, as earlier argued, is probably not authorial. When we come to the arrangement of smaller groups of poems, however, we are on firmer ground. The consecutive numbering from 1 to 70 followed by Cranstoun in his edition has, in the manuscript, been added by a later hand. The original numbering marks out only short sequences, varying in length from two sonnets to five and almost certainly transmitting the intentions of the author. Cranstoun does not print these more important numbers, preferring to use invented titles ('To the Same'; 'On the Same') to mark out boundaries. He does, however, on two occasions err, giving 'A Ladyis Lamentatione' six sonnets instead of three and treating 'Of the Duleweid' as the first in a series which does not exist. Sometimes too his invented titles may prove rather misleading to the unwary. By labelling two groups of love poems 'To his Maistres' and 'On his Maistres' he tacitly assumes a real involvement on the poet's part, when the works in question might equally well be conventional exercises.

These mini-sequences mingle with single sonnets and although they do not form any neat analytic order, certain broad thematic groupings can be traced here, as in the Ker MS as a whole. Within the outermost circle of sonnets which directly or indirectly proclaim spiritual values there come poems relating to the poet's life in both its public and its private aspects. Early in the collection a number of complimentary sonnets written in his capacity as 'maister poete' dominate. They are followed by a very impressive group of complaints personal and dramatic. These include those tracing the pension debate, an extended appeal to Robert Hudson and 'A Ladyis Lamentatione'. Towards the end of the collection the public poems are defences rather than eulogies and the personal ones present a more easygoing, at times Bacchanalian, outlook. Separating these groups and thus again structurally at the centre of the arrangement come the sonnets dealing with love. Although some of these are also set off in groups there is no overall ordering principle and many of the poems in the section are commissioned works written in praise of leading figures at Court. Although they express love, these are essentially Occasional verses having as much in common with the eulogies as with more serious amatory writing. Once more, however, worldly love is set within a form which frames it with the trials of earthly existence and ultimately refers both to divine values.

If we look first at the love sonnets, our initial task is to re-define the limits of the section as outlined by Hoffmann.[12] As 'A Ladyis Lamentatione' finishes at S XXXV, the following three sonnets open the love section rather than concluding the Lady's tragic tale. The original numbering reveals them to be a unified group of three. As such they are undeniably expressions of Petrarchan love, dealing respectively with the passion's paradoxicality, the lover's inability to break free from his grief in fact or fantasy and those aspects of his nature which are to blame for his despair.

In the discussion of the love lyric, it was noted that Montgomerie sometimes adapted the Petrarchan vision with verve and ingenuity but sometimes merely echoed the (by now conventional) ideas of the Italian. These sonnets fall into the latter category. Each relies to a greater or lesser degree on a listing technique reinforced by initial repetition. The imagery of fleeing yet courting love's fire, of embarking on the voyage of life or of inadequately defending oneself with love's shield is traditional and not reinterpreted in any important way. Montgomerie's usual verbal ingenuity is also lacking and what we have are three neat but unremarkable restatements of a well-known literary vision of love.

Generally speaking those sonnets which express the emotion in courtly, Petrarchan terms are less successful than the equivalent lyrics. There are of course moments

when linguistic skill or tonal variation breaks through
convention. S LI, 'To The for Me', for example, is based on
the traditional idea of the Nightingale singing in pain but
its cries are cleverly expressed using alliteration and
onomatopoeia:

quivering trills   Thy chivring chirlis whilks changinglie
                    thou [chants]   (S LI, 3)

and the narrator's exasperated protest

innocent; guiltless   . . . thou sees not, sillie, saikles thing,
prick   The peircing pykis brods at thy bony
                    breist!   (S LI, 7–8)

creates a memorable note of pent-up frustration.

But the vast majority of the poems in this section are
'poeticall exercises' of one sort or another—conventional
expressions of Petrarchism, commissioned eulogies designed to demonstrate the poet's wit or skilful Ronsardian imitations. The personal note is not strong, a fact
which makes Cranstoun's invented 'mistress' titles even
more misleading than they might otherwise have been.

The definition of love, then, is a broad one. The sonnet
form is well adapted for courtly compliments and the
'maister poete' dutifully uses it to recognise exceptional
beauty and marriages at Court. Usually these works are
remarkable mainly for their stylistic ingenuity, complex
verse forms or a witty, underlying conceit. They are
eulogies whose chosen focus is love; at once serious, yet
'jeux d'esprit' celebrating both the courtier's fame and
Montgomerie's artistry. Thus Isabella Young's marriage
is given public recognition in a sonnet using 'vers
enchayenné':

intend   Prove when 3e pleis, I mynd not to
                    rem[ove;]
decree   Remove who may if Destinies decreit:
                  Decreit is given by Hymen high above;
                  Above all bands that blissed band is
                    sweet,   (S XLIII, 5–8)

while Johne Johnson and Jane Maxwell are rewarded with
the complex caesura rhymes of 'rime batelée:

> Good love is gone except my love alone,
> Thoght gromes can grone as they wald   fellows
>   give the ghost;
> Half mang'd almost als stupefact as   bewildered
>   stone,
> Lyk treuth in throne, they look as they
>   wer lost.
>
> (S XLV, 5–8)

Witty wordplay often centres round the lady's name and
may take many forms. For example, the opening phrase of
S XLIV, 'Treu fame we mis', contains the name of one of
the leading ladies at Court, Eufame Wemis; while the
identity of Margaret Douglas, a relation of the poet, is
cryptically presented in three stages. She is the pearl or
"MARGARET . . . jem of jewels", whom the poet wishes
to tame like a turtle dove (DOU) in a cage of glass
(GLAS). Even the name of the poet's own 'mistress' is
presented in riddle form:

> Quhat pregnant sprit the letters can
>   espy
> My ladyis name and surname that
>   begins?
> Betwixt thame (ay) in ordour is bot I
> And only I these lovely letters twins.   separates
>
> (S XLVI, 1–4)

One would deduce that the initials concerned are H.J.,
especially as the poet advises his readers in the final
couplet:

> Or ȝe this find, I feir ȝe first be fane
> For to begin your A.B.C. agane.
>
> (S XLVI, 13–14)

This enthusiasm for disguising names has led some
critics to see S XLII as a veiled statement of the poet's

Marian sympathies. Addressed to a known supporter of
the queen—James Lauder—its opening lines are open to
two interpretations:

> I wald se mare nor ony thing I sie;
> I sie not ʒit the thing that I desyre.
>
> (S XLII, 1–2)

The rhythm and lack of capitalisation encourage a reading
of 'mare' as meaning more. But if Lauder understood
'Mare' (Mary) instead, then the poem becomes a warning
that any action to save the queen must be undertaken
hastily:

> I dreid no thing bot ouer long delay.
> Delay in love is dangerous indeid.
>
> (S XLII, 10–11)

and promises the poet's active support:

come   Assay I sall, hap ill or weill I vow.
trust   I vow to ventur, to triumph I trow.

> (S XLII, 13–14)

Even if this sonnet has a concealed political meaning, it
still makes its surface appeal through wordplay, stylistic
ingenuity and mastery of 'vers enchayenné'.

    All the Ronsardian imitations are also contained in this
section. Sometimes they have been adapted to form part
of a sustained mini-sequence along with original works.
For example, the original numbering sets off Sonnets
LIV–LVIII as a separate group. It begins with two
original sonnets in which the poet appeals to the Muses for
inspiration in praising the lady and outlines the miseries of
his suit through conceits based on archery and legal
procedure. All this naturally leads into a philosophical
débate with Plato in which the poet maintains that the
voids around earth must be filled by the air of his sighs and
the water of his tears. The argument is Ronsard's in
'Pardonne moy, Platon, si je ne cuide' and throughout the

octet Montgomerie follows the original closely. In the sestet, however, he adopts a much freer approach and ends by emphasising not his likely death but a possible rescue by sympathetic heavenly powers.

This indirect reference to the pagan gods enables him to make a neat transition, involving the 'change of purposis' advocated by James. What if one God is not sympathetic but implacably opposed to him?

> Wha wald behold him whom a god so
>   grievis?
> Whom he assaild and danton'd with his   subdued
>   [dairt]
> Of whom he freizis and inflams the
>   hairt,
> Whais shame siclyk him gritest honour   similarly
>   givis.
>
>   (S LVII, 1–4)

What Montgomerie has done here is to depart from close imitation of one Ronsardian sonnet in order to draw in another as part of a continuous argument. The four lines quoted imitate closely the opening quatrain of the first sonnet in the *Amours*:

> Qui voudra voyr comme un Dieu me
>   surmonte
> Comme il m'assault, comme il se fait
>   vainqueur,
> Comme il r'enflamme, & r'englace mon
>   cuoeur,
> Comme il reçoit un honneur de ma
>   honte.[13]

Montgomerie's skills as an imitator are not therefore confined to variations within single sonnets. Sometimes specific adaptations are favoured so that a consistent line of thought may emerge. In this instance 'Qui voudra voyr' provides further evidence of Love's power and picks up the

imagery of Cupid's bow earlier referred to in S LV. In turn
it acts as a fitting prelude to the impassioned questioning of
the last (original) sonnet:

murder

        How long sall Love, but mercy, murther
          me?
        How long against me sall his bow be
          bent?   (S LVIII, 3–4)

with its final use of Underwriting to propose a brave
rearguard action against Cupid's dominance:

reinstate
fortune;
health

        Revenge, revert, revive, revest, reveall,
        My hurt, my hairt, my hope, my hap,
          my heall.   (S LVIII, 13–14)

While it is true, therefore, that Sonnets XXXVI–LXI
are all in one sense or another amatory, variety is again the
keynote. In particular quite a large number are commissioned compliments and so have strong links with the
eulogies to which I now turn. Most of these appear early in
the MS, preceding both the complaints and the love
poetry. When considering them it is important to note that
this was, in James's view, the main purpose for the sonnet.
He himself used the form to extol people as diverse as Sir
Philip Sidney and Tycho Brahe. But of course he also
anticipated praise for himself and his writings from
members of the Castalian entourage. Montgomerie was
quick to appreciate this, using the sonnet to flatter his
monarch in two different ways.

The first was direct praise. The 'maister poete' regularly
hymned James's qualities as ruler, man and poet, but
nowhere so fully nor so successfully as in the sonnets
praising the king's version of Du Bartas' *Uranie*. In *The
Essayes of a Prentise* all five writers who contribute
vernacular sonnets link the king and his verse with the
pagan gods and the muses. Presumably they had been told
to use this mythological apparatus because James had
employed it in his own introductory verses. Montgomerie

is represented by the single sonnet 'Can goldin Titan schyning bright at morne' and the aptness of associating the poet-king with the leader of the Muses and centre of universal harmony needs no re-stressing. What the Ker MS reveals, however, is that this poem was only one in a numbered sequence of four sonnets unified by this equation between James and the Sun God. 'Can goldin Titan' is the third and presumably was chosen by James. Presented in isolation, its relation to the rest of the group is lost.

In the first 'Uranie' sonnet Montgomerie's emphasis is on Apollo as the light which shines through darkness, putting to shame his pale sister Diana. In the same way, James's version of Du Bartas' poem brings to us the light of knowledge and overshadows other writers. Then the emphasis changes. 'Of Titan's harp', as the opening phrase suggests, is concerned with Apollo in his rôle as leader of the muses and bringer of harmony. In the same way, the music of James's verse is superior to that of his followers.[14] Despite his youth he makes the Castalians painfully aware of their "fordullit hedes" and "blunter branes". This is the immediate context of 'Can goldin Titan' here cited as it appears not in *The Essayes* but in Ker:

Can goldin Titan shyning bright at morne	
For light of torches cast a gritter shaw?	show
Can thunder reird the higher for a horne?	roar
Craks cannouns louder thoght a cok suld craw?	
Can our waik breathis help Boreas to blaw?	
Can candle low give fyr a griter heet?	flame
Can quhytest swanis more quhyter mak the snaw?	
Can virgins teirs augment the winter['s weet?]	

Helps pyping Pan Apollo's musik sweet?
Can fontans smal the ocean sea incres?
No! They augment the griter not a
whit   quheet
Bot they thame selfis appeir to grow
      the les.
So, peirles Prince, thy cunning maks the
      knowne.
stain   Ours helps not thyn; we stein3ie bot our
      awne.

                                    (S XII)

The series of parallels demonstrates that minor forces do
not augment major ones but only call attention to their
own inadequacy. This neatly complements the earlier
argument and although the poet produces a list of
comparisons Titan/Apollo still dominates, opening both
octet and sestet. But it is now his power which most
impresses, while the final reference to staining provides a
verbal link with the last poem in the group, 'As bright
Apollo staineth eviry star'. Here all three attributes are
brought together. James/Apollo illuminates, creates order
and makes others shrink away in fear. But an alternative
parallel is also introduced. By likening the king to the
phoenix, Montgomerie calls attention not only to his
uniqueness but anticipates the title of the other major
poem in *The Essayes*, James's elegy on Esmé Stuart and
welcome to his son, Ludovick.[15]

   He finds an even more subtle way of flattering his
monarch in S IX. This time the object of praise is Maitland
of Thirlestane. The work, written in 1587, links the
Chancellor's virtues to those of Mars, Minerva, Mercury
and the Muses. One year earlier the king had used the
same structure and comparisons in his complimentary
sonnet to Sir Philip Sidney. The only variation in detail is
Montgomerie's substitution of Minerva for Apollo, almost
certainly because he wished to reserve the latter for praise

of the king alone. In imitating his Maecenas, the senior poet once more flatters him.

> A cunning king a cunning chanceller   wise
>   chuisis.
>
> (S IX, 8)

Indeed he even contrives to make Maitland's wisdom an aspect of James's. Unfortunately a comparison between the two also serves to underline Montgomerie's superior craftsmanship. His work is much more powerful, partly because he uses alliteration to force home his points and adopts a simple syntax rather than James's complex, Latinate one. But he also lays more emphasis on the number four:

> Quhais fourfald force with furie him   whose
>   infusis
> In battells, counsels, orisones and brain, speeches
>
> (S IX, 5–6)

and suggests the numerological connection between that number and the ideas of order and human strength. Maitland's power is thus doubly underlined, using a technique which the king himself admired, having learned it from his idol, Du Bartas.

In later years, as we have noted, Montgomerie came to regret the extravagance of these compliments to James. But it can only be the message and not the manner which troubled him. As a eulogist he does not miss a trick, the only irony being that in describing so masterfully how the king's verse eclipses his own he demonstrates to any careful critic the exact opposite. Nor are his comments on writing confined to these brilliant but intentionally sycophantic works. Immediately after the love sonnets comes a much shorter group of three sonnets, which to some degree redress the balance and suggest a rather different approach to verse and attitude to authority.

Sonnets LXII to LXIV are all apologies in the old sense

of defence by argument. Addressed respectively to the Kirk of Edinburgh, to an anonymous writer and to the king, they assume varying tones of defiance and use techniques which would not be out of place in a flyting. They each start from the assumption that the arch-eulogiser also has a reputation for bitter satire. This has led those in power to suppose he was the author of scurrilous works, which now he vehemently disowns. In disclaiming them variously on the grounds that any work of his would have been much more blistering than the one credited to him; that he would not handle so unworthy a theme and that he would never attack the dead, he shows a scorn for authority almost as extreme as the idolisation of the eulogies. The tone varies from the condescending irony with which he addresses the Kirk:

> I wonder of ȝour Wisdomes that ar wyse
> misunderstand   That baith miskennis my method and
>   my muse;
>
> (S LXII, 1–2)

through disgust at a poet who could malign Edinburgh's maidens:

> Quhat madnes mov'd such venemous
>   words to [write?]
> Quhat hellish hands hes led they bluidie
>   pen?
>
> (S LXIII, 5–6)

to a dignified protestation of innocence for James:

> Sir, I am sorie that ȝe suld suppone
> Me to be one in lucre to delyte
> Or spew despyt against hir who is gone.
>
> (S LXIV, 1–3)

Here is the other side of the coin. A professional poet knows his place at court and will bolster the egos of the powerful as part of his contract. But if his artistic integrity

is questioned, his poetic skills undervalued, then that
power over words which glorifies may also destroy:

> For if I open up my anger anes
> To plunge my pen into that stinking
>   Styx,
> My tongue is lyk the lyons—whair it liks
> It brings the flesh, lyk bryrie, fra the   *briars*
>   banes.
>
>   (S LXII, 9–12)

And there can be little doubt that, although Montgomerie
could match most lyricists and sonneteers in celebrating
love or honouring the great, he really comes into his own
when using these forms as a vehicle for satire, flyting
complaint or petition. To confirm this we need only turn to
the sequences which can fairly be said to dominate the
sonnet section—those concerned with his pension and
rejection from Court.

Those specifically concerned with his pension resemble a
diary, tracing his thoughts and feelings throughout the
long case. Addressed to James, to the Lords of Session and
to the lawyers for prosecution and defence their tonal
movement from deference to fury gives us a touching
insight into the poet's earlier hopes and later despair.
Always at his best when adopting a specific dramatic
rôle—in this case the innocent assailed by authority—
Montgomerie has the artistry to change over and over
again his mode of approach from flattery to rational
argument to passionate appeal to bitter satire and to direct
insult. All the poetic lessons he learned in the 'games' of
masque, flyting and courtly 'making' generally are
harnessed in this attempt to rescue, through words, his
pension and position.

The four sonnets to James show this process most clearly.
In the MS they immediately follow the overgenerous
praising of the king's *Uranie* (also a group of four) and this
placing adds poignancy to the contrast in situation. Montgomerie opens with a rational appeal, using opposed

phrases to protest that his erstwhile patron is not the true
object of his anger:

> Help, Prince, to whom, on whom not I
>   complene,
> But on, not to fals fortun, ay my fo;
> Quha but, not by a resone reft me fro;
> Quho did, not does, ʒit suld my self
>   sustene.
>
> (S XIV, 1–4)

The rôle is one of continued belief in friendship and the
work ends with a simple appeal that his pension be
restored. In the next sonnet both mood and method have
changed. The petition is now an emotional one and the
rejected 'maister poete' in adopting a tone of righteous
indignation, uses initial repetition and classical parallels
forcefully to present himself as a worthy writer wrongfully
neglected. James's innocence is no longer assumed.
Implicitly as Maecenas he stands convicted of ignoring
talent and leaving his senior poet as "lukles" as Virgil
(somewhat inappropriately), Ovid and Homer. The third
poem uses many of the same rhetorical devices but finally
moves the centre of blame from Fortune to James himself.
It is more specific in focus, mentioning details of the case
and while the poet is still consciously standing on his
dignity he also cleverly builds up to a climax of anger in the
third quatrain before dropping to the quieter note of the
final couplet:

> Is this the frute, Sir, of your first
>   affectione—
> My pensioun perish under your
>   protectio[ne?]
>
> (S XVI, 13–14)

That sudden change from the anger of exclamation to a
simple question revealing at once incredulity and vulnerability is a master stroke. It conveys the poet's pride and
helplessness but above all it reveals his deep pain in

contemplating what William Mow has now done to his 'belovit Sanders'.

Montgomerie does not allow himself any further flirtations with self-pity. Instead the final sonnet bids a manly farewell to king and Court:

> Adeu my King, court, cuntrye and my
>   kin,
> Adeu swete Duke whose father held me
>   deir,
> Adeu companiones Constable and Keir
> Thrie trewar hairts I trow sall never
>   twin.   (S XVII, 1–4)

The focus of his appeal is still James but in widening his farewell to include friends who have not let him down, Montgomerie adds to the finality of 'Adeu' a contrast between loyalty and treachery which works against James. In the following two quatrains he enacts their estrangement by speaking only to his true friends and referring to the king in the third person. The final shot is reserved for the couplet:

> Sen wryt nor wax nor word is not a word   writing; promise
> I must perforce ga seik my fathers sword.
>   (S XVII, 13–14)

The direct reference to ignored petitions and broken agreements is one of the most outspoken condemnations of James in Montgomerie's verse and the proverb which follows intentionally leaves the poet's intentions vague. Does he seek vengeance or suicide? Or has the proverb its more usual connotations of one bound on a journey with no set destination or likelihood of success?

These sonnets are almost unbearably affecting, as they doubtless were meant to be. They are also among the most skilfully designed petitions known to me in any language. Inevitably the other pension groups are not so personal but in their own way they are just as carefully 'made' and exhibit a similar range of tone and technique. The Lords of Session are wooed with flattery at the beginning of the case and consigned to Hell at the end. Montgomerie attempts to disarm them with wordplay and frighten them with thoughts of a higher judgement. He even tries to match them at their own game, proposing legal arguments which, no matter how interpreted, point to his pension being restored. But for his own Advocate, Sharpe, earlier complimented on his agile intellect by a pun on his name, there is reserved the only outright piece of flyting in the whole group:

baker's progeny; babbler	A baxters bird, a bluiter beggar borne,
falsely baptised bastard	Ane ill heud huirsone lyk a barkit hyde,
scoundrel; perjured	A saulles swinger, sevintie tymes men001sworne,
paltry coward	A peltrie pultron poyson'd up with pryde.　　　　(S XXIV, 1–4)

If the 'pension' sonnets resemble a diary, the five addressed to Montgomerie's successor as 'maister poete' Robert Hudson suggest a continuous letter.[16] They must have been written prior to 1595 for they mention as a living poet Robert Semple, who died in that year. They probably postdate the Court's decision in 1593, and certainly deal with the days of Montgomerie's exile from Court. He hopes to use Hudson as a go-between with James and ends with the appeal that he

> Shaw to the King this poor complant of myne.

With Hudson, Montgomerie can be as personal as he had been with his royal friend. He also feels that he can drop the manly dignity and depict his state in more pathetic terms, referring to his illness, loneliness and longing for the cultural companionship of the Castalians:

My bestbelovit brother of the band,
I grein to sie the sillie smiddy smeik.   long; smithy smoke
This is no lyfe that I live upaland   in the country
On raw rid herring reistit in the reik,   dried; smoke
Syn I am subject somtyme to be seik
And daylie deing of my auld diseis,   dying
Eit breid, ill aill and all things on ane eik,   in a greasy state
This barme and blaidry buists up all my   yeast; filth; box-up;
    bees.   fancies

(S XXV, 1–8)

The intention is clear. Using Hudson, Montgomerie can convey to the king in more vivid and desperate manner the horror of his new situation. Thus, although he is careful to praise the other poet in glowing terms, it is his continued love for the king which is the major topic. He recalls earlier days and specifically his flyting victory, when he "chaist Polwart from the chimney [nuik]". He likens himself to the well-meaning ass in Aesop whose attempts to mimic the actions of a lapdog resulted in unfair punishment and protests that he had no designs on political power being merely a love poet.

In short, the once proud 'maister poete' grovels. He does so with all his usual rhetorical versatility but the extreme lengths to which he is prepared to go in seeking re-instatement underline his despair. The sonnet addressed to Hudson by Christen Lyndesay, the only female poet associated with the Castalians, confirms that his loss of pride was rewarded only by further proof of fickle friendship:

> Montgomerie, that such hope did once
>   conceave
> Of thy guid-will, now finds all is
>   forgotten.
> Thoght not bot kyndnes he did at the
>   craiv,
> He finds thy freindship as it rypis is
>   rotten.   (S XXX, 9–12)

Having discussed Montgomerie's powerful use of the sonnet form for dramatic personal complaints, I must also mention the one series in which he 'complains' using a different persona. 'A Ladyis Lamentatione' comes shortly after the Hudson sonnets. If the earlier groups had the form of diary or letter, these three sonnets constitute a dramatic monologue. The lady, like Montgomerie, has fallen from high estate and the opening sonnet in particular, with its attack on Fate and its reference to false early promises of worldly success, is reminiscent of 'Ane Invectione against Fortun' and 'The Poets Complaint of his Nativitie'.

Montgomerie shares with Burns the ability to empathise with his creations and these poems are among his finest. The lady at the end of the first sonnet sees herself as another Cressida and it is this parallel which is developed in the second. Like Henryson she emphasises Cressida's worldliness, the ugliness caused by her leprosy and the fear that her story may become known in verse or song. The second parallel with the owl complements the first, for the owl too is ugly, exiled and shuns the light. By the end of the poem she reaches a nadir of despair, seeing no escape in life or death.

For Montgomerie in his complaints there is no comforting solution. For the lady there is. In a manner which anticipates Milton, the last movement solves the insoluble by moving from a temporal to a spiritual frame of reference. Self-pity gives way to penance; physical disease is discounted when she thinks of the divine healer and the misery which can find consolation neither in life nor death turns to joy at the prospect of salvation:

> My swete Redemer, let me never die
> But blink on me even with Thy blisful
> b[emes.]

(S XXXV, 10–11)

Even the depressing obsession with Cressida is transcended

for she thinks now not of pagan tragedy but of Christian
redemption:

> And mak another Magdalene of me.
> Forgive my gylt, sen nane bot God is
>   gude.
> So, with 'Peccavi Pater' I conclude.   'I have sinned,
>   father'

(S XXXV, 12–14)

Without doubt these rather different 'complaint'
sequences are the most powerful and memorable of the
sonnets in the Ker MS. In suggesting their superiority
either to the love sonnets or even the most ingenious of the
eulogies, I am not betraying a preference for more direct
and personal verse. It is Montgomerie who finds his true
fulfilment as a lyrical writer when his skills as a makar unite
with dramatic situation and passionate concern. Personal
involvement does not, for him, produce uncontrolled self-
indulgent verse. It challenges his professionalism and
reveals even further his mastery over words and ideas.

Yet our study cannot end here. Just as the eulogies were
partly counterpointed by the apologies, so the complaints
with their pessimistic view of life, fortune and false
friendship are also partly counterpointed by a later group
(S LXV–LXIX) defying fortune and celebrating true
friendship. As these, like the apologies, follow the love
sonnets they confirm the rough circular form and, more
importantly, they provide a last example of the poet's
stylistic range.

They strike a new and uncharacteristically optimistic
note. Two are by his friend Hugh Barclay of Ladyland but
all five stress the value of personal friendship in an
unfriendly world. Written at different periods in the
author's career, they seem to have been placed together
because they share this theme and give us an insight into
that convivial side to his nature which had impressed the
youthful James. The intimacy of the subject matter is

reflected in a colloquial style involving a much heavier use of Scots words than usual and S LXIX ('The Old Maister') in particular anticipates that glorification of drink as a temporary 'bield' to be found in Fergusson's 'Daft Days' or Burns's 'The Jolly Beggars'. Somehow it seems fitting to end this introduction to his sonnets with the poet for once dismissing his inveterate enemy 'Dame Fortun' and finding some comradeship in a life which had known so much disloyalty.

	The Lesbian Lad that weirs the wodbind w[reath]
gladdens; company	With Ceres and Cylenus gled your ging.
	Be blyth Kilburnie with the Bairns of Be[ath]
	And let Lochwinnoch Lordie lead ʒour ri[ng.]
	Be mirrie men, feir God and serve the K[ing]
enmity	And cair not by Dame Fortuns fead a fl[ea.]
	Syne welcome hame swete Semple, sie ʒe sin[g,]
	Gut ou'r and let the wind shute in the s[ea.]
	I, Richie, Jane and George are lyk to d[ee,]
gossiping	Four crabit crippilis crackand in our crouch.
interpreter	Sen I am trensh-man for the other thri[e,]
	Let drunken Pancrage drink to me in D[utch.]
Skol! (cheers!); burst	Scol frie, al out, albeit that I suld brist
	Ih wachts, hale beir, fan hairts and nych[sum] drist.[17]

(S LXIX)

NOTES

1. I have accepted Ladyland's view that S LXVII, although attributed to Ezechiel Montgomery, is in fact by the 'maister poete'. Although listed among the sonnets, both it and Ladyland's reply are sixteen lines long.
2. Stevenson, *Poems of Montgomerie*, *op. cit.*, pp. 218–22.
3. See *A Choice of Scottish Verse, 1470–1570*, ed. John and Winifred MacQueen, London, 1972, p. 139, p. 203.
4. R. H. MacDonald, *The Library of Drummond of Hawthornden*. Edinburgh, 1971, p. 24.
5. *Poems of James*, *op. cit.*, I, 81.
6. R. D. S. Jack, "Petrarch in English and Scottish Literature", *Modern Language Review*, 71, 1976, pp. 801–11.
7. Oscar Hoffman, *Studien zu Alexander Montgomerie*, Altenburg, 1894, pp. 19–22.
8. Brotanek, *op. cit.*, pp. 117–18.
9. Shire, *Song, Dance and Poetry*, *op. cit.*, pp. 150–8.
10. *Ibid.*, p. 150.
11. As argued by Brian Jeffery, "The idea of Music in Ronsard's poetry" in *Ronsard the Poet*, ed. Terence Cave. London, 1973, p. 218.
12. Hoffmann, *op. cit.*, p. 16. He would begin the section at S XXXVIII and end at S LXI.
13. *Les Amours de Ronsard*, ed. H. and C. Weber, Paris, 1963, p. 4.
14. Here Montgomerie certainly uses musical terms as a metaphor for poetry. The king had little musical knowledge and the *Uranie* was not set to music.
15. *Works of James*, *op. cit.*, *Ane Metaphoricall Invention of a Tragedie Called Phoenix*, I, 39–59.
16. As noted by Mrs Shire in *Song, Dance and Poetry*, *op. cit.*, p. 150.
17. The general sense of the last line seems to be "Plenty of drink, good beer, fond hearts and a huge thirst".

CHAPTER V

THE CHERRIE AND THE SLAE

Almost all the work we have been considering so far was known to a limited, predominantly courtly group and existed only in manuscript form. The major exception to this rule is the lengthy allegorical poem, *The Cherrie and the Slae*, which went through so many reprints during the seventeenth and eighteenth centuries that then it ranked second in popularity only to Blind Hary's *Wallace*. Remaining true to his preference for complex metrical forms, Montgomerie chose the fourteen-line stanza with bob and wheel which Ramsay was later to adopt in *The Vision* and Burns in the Recitativo of *The Jolly Beggars*. As the allegory is itself a complex one, the poet confronts a double challenge, while laying himself open to criticisms such as that advanced by Pinkerton—"The stanza is good for a song, but the worst in the world for a long poem."[1] C. S. Lewis on the other hand thinks it is the "beautiful stanza" which "saves" the work: "In Montgomerie we seem to hear the scrape of the fiddle and the beat of dancing on the turf."[2] It is indeed possible that the poem, despite its length, was meant to be sung. Precedents for musical settings to long poems exist. Even the *Orlando Furioso* had a setting which matched its stanza and editions of *The Cherrie and the Slae* are usually accompanied by the sprightly tune 'About the Bankis of Helicon', which had recently been given a new setting for four voices by Blackhall.[3] Montgomerie handles the stanza confidently and whether the work is viewed as being sung, spoken aloud, or studied on the printed page, I can only see the chosen form as enhancing the message.

As will be seen, the allegory is at times subtle and the symbolism employed not always precise. As a result, the poem has been valued (and dismissed) through the ages for very different reasons and assuming very different authorial intentions. It is not my purpose to give a full critical background, but it is helpful to identify the four major schools of thought. Some earlier critics, for example, laid great stress on the proverbial wisdom it contained and so regarded it as a sort of encyclopedia or "magazine of pithy witt".[4] C. S. Lewis and others have seen it as an erotic allegory stemming from *The Romance of the Rose*. This places it at the very end of a tradition which, in Lewis's own terms, "has taken an unconscionable time to die".[5] Considered against the background of a Scottish renaissance which aimed at looking forward, this seems odd. The majority of commentators would point to a wider moral and/or religious significance. This line, which would link the poem with a newer, more flourishing tradition having Scottish precedents in Douglas's *King Hart* and Rolland's *Court of Venus*, begins with the comments of Dempster in the early seventeenth century. Essentially he sees it as a love allegory between high-born and humble mistress which also has a divine message.[6] Of those who accept this premise, some feel with Cranstoun that the movement from one level to another is poorly handled, so that "a love piece" changes awkwardly into a "moral poem".[7] Others, notably Ian Ross, do not admit such a dislocation and stress the poem's religious significance.[8] Mrs Shire, the poem's most thorough critic, accepts most of Ross's findings but lays stress on Montgomerie's Catholic leanings and the symbolism of 'Cherrie' and 'Slae' to argue for a more specific religious interpretation, involving an opposition between Catholicism and Protestantism.[9]

All but the first of these critical groups work with the consciousness that the poem is at different stages and to different degrees indebted to a variety of earlier literary traditions. As Ross remarks, "To read *The Cherrie and the*

Slae, or to hear it, is to experience something of the enduring culture of Europe".[10] This is true. It is at once a dream vision and a love adventure in spring, reliant at points on the argument and characters of *The Romance of the Rose*. It is also a debate which uses techniques drawn from the internal soul-battle as illustrated by Prudentius' *Psychomachia*, and from that branch of the 'conflictus' which focuses attention on non-human contestants of the same natural order and includes works such as "The Violet and the Rose". To these I would add another, the poem of spiritual instruction, which, like *The Pearl*, takes the dreaming narrator from ignorance to knowledge by a combination of vision and argument. In such works the allegorical implications of both discussion and symbols may alter and deepen as the poem progresses and the dreamer learns.

I stress this, not only because *The Cherrie and the Slae* cannot be approached in a historical vacuum, but because reliance on analogues has to be carefully controlled. Montgomerie, as usual, comes to traditions partly to benefit from them, partly to redefine them and place them in a new, unique combination. Too heavy a reliance on the logic of any one tradition without noting the ways in which the poet handles it will lead to false critical emphases. These in turn may lead us either to accuse him of not doing well what he was not trying to do at all or to accrete significances, valid only if he were following the convention in a more slavish manner than is his wont. My analysis, therefore, will attempt to discuss the meaning of the poem in relation to the poet's use of these conventions; to discover which are given the greatest weight and so to assess the validity or otherwise of interpretations which highlight one or other.

It is first necessary, however, to know something about the composition of the poem and the editorial problems involved. Although much of the work was circulating in MS form during the early 1580s, it only reached print in an unfinished and currupt form, published by Waldegrave in 1597. Later that year, the same publisher brought out a corrected edition, but the complete poem did not appear until 1615 under Andro Hart's imprint. This version added 47 stanzas to the earlier print but unfortunately no copy of it remains. In 1636 Wreittoun published what is in all likelihood a reprint of Hart's text. This last edition was the one followed in the seventeenth and eighteenth centuries and is the text which I shall be following as I am sure that it comes closest to the author's final intentions. In it he adds the lessons of experience and carefully revises the earlier work in ways which have been fully discussed elsewhere.[11] Essentially these alterations strengthen the thematic unity of the piece; make the tone of the opening Spring day description less joyful than before; alter the significance of Cupid and add a debate between Reason and Will. The reasons for these changes will be covered in the analysis which follows.

The Celebration of May

The first seven stanzas are at first sight a conventional description of May, with the dreamer[12] lying on a bank, celebrating the beauties of Nature. All levels are described—animals, birds, plants—with the emphasis, foreseeably, on love and procreation. He sees a river coursing through the countryside and specifically notes a waterfall plunging down from a steep rock. So impressed is he, indeed, that he wishes a poet capable of mastering a higher "heroick" style could take over from him and "pen the pleasures of that parke".

All this—the joyous May setting and the modesty topos—are just what we would expect as a prelude to a love adventure. But closer attention reveals a tension between the sensual joy of the dreamer and the evidence being used to back it up. The three major mythological parallels adduced concern Progne, Echo and Apollo. These do not suggest joyous, fulfilled love but—respectively—rape, self-love and the misery derived from faithlessness. Even at this stage we sense that the Narrator, while describing his youthful reaction to the scene, may be doing so from a position of greater knowledge, which is acting as a corrective to his earlier joy.

Also, while love and fertility remain firmly at the centre of the picture, they do not define Nature and the wider vision confirms the suspicion that all is not harmony and light. The birds, instead of singing tunefully, "pratle, jangle, craik and keckle", producing such a noise that even the hopeful dreamer is forced to admit that "They deav'd me with their din". The presence too of backbiting magpies, lamenting turtle doves and the proud peacock reflect a community in which cruelty, rivalry and disappointment are more evident than the joyous companionship which might have been anticipated.

The animals are not so obviously divided but the presence amongst them of the "false foxe" and a hunter with "subtile snares" introduces connotations of evil and devilishness drawn from bestiary and fable.[13] At all levels one senses an opposition between the immediately attractive appearance of things and a much darker reality. Thus the plants appeal to the senses of sight and smell, but their beauty is enhanced by the dew shed in misery by the deserted lovers of Apollo and their "heavy heads declinde" suggest a sympathetic misery much at odds with the sensual joy of the dreamer viewing them. The bees too are hailed ecstatically as Nature's alchemists and types of profitable labour but closer analysis reveals that this constant activity is made necessary by a Nature which presents them with the alternatives of theft or starvation.

Montgomerie has, therefore, employed the convention of the dreamer welcoming a joyous May scene, a situation which often leads into the description of an amorous adventure. And, on cue, Cupid arrives. But the scene he enters is one which has introduced issues other than love, while stressing the conflicts and miseries veiled by the attractive appearance of Nature generally. The dreamer evaluates through the senses and so emphasises the positive side of the picture. Already, however, the reader senses that his optimism may be that of youth, recalled by a more experienced Narrator. Certainly, his vision is an ignorant and earthly one and his welcoming of the sound of the river as harmonious and heavenly has to be evaluated within that context.

THE INTERVENTION OF CUPID AND ITS EFFECT

The initial background has prepared us for a general, rather than solely erotic, allegory; drawn a clear distinction between Nature's lovely appearance and a much starker reality; and introduced a youth badly in need of counsel. On to this stage comes Cupid. Stanzas 8–26 tell how he is welcomed by the dreamer and offers him his wings and arrows. These are hurriedly accepted and the dreamer sets off. Two things go wrong. He flies too high and he aims badly, wounding himself rather than "another". On his return Cupid first mocks, then deserts him, takes back his gear and returns to the heavens. The wound makes him feel Courage and Desire, which inflame his heart. Dominated by fire (i.e. only one of the four elements which harmoniously make up man's nature) he inevitably falls ill and in that state sees for the first time the two fruits which give the poem its title. On a tree growing high on a crag are the beautiful cherries. Much lower down is a bush of bitter sloes. Both stand on the far side of the river, which earlier he had described. Instinctively he longs for the cherries but sees no practical way of reaching them and so remains in a state of indecision.

It is helpful to look in turn at the three situations within this section—the meeting with Cupid; the illness; and the 'fruitful' vision. But at the outset it must be made clear that the dominant line throughout is 'erotic'. Cupid is traditionally God of love. The dreamer's heart is set on fire and that fire is kept going by "loves bellowes". If one thinks at this stage of the Cherrie and the Slae as representing respectively inaccessible and more easily attainable loves, these ideas are in accord with the poem's current emphasis.

But it is only an emphasis. The allegory is not as simple as this and Montgomerie is still using the underlying conventions imaginatively. First, we have confirmation that the Narrator's voice is that of experience looking back on earlier errors. While the dreamer welcomes Cupid with unreserved enthusiasm, the Narrator comments:

behaviour   Perceiving mine having,
                         He counted me his prey,

                                                    (9/13–14)

and wryly regrets

fear   Of doublenesse I had no doubt.

                                                    (10/2)

The two voices, implicitly opposed in the May description, now reveal themselves as those of youth being recalled in the greater wisdom of age, a conclusion which may account for the time the poet took to complete this, his major work, and his initial presentation of it in uncompleted form.

The youth's ignorance reveals itself throughout the Cupid episode, but first it is necessary to define the rôle of the God himself. To begin with, he is called by two names—not only Cupid but Cupido. The latter is Latin for 'desire' and the temptation he represents clearly covers not only worldly love but worldly desires generally. Faced with an ignorant but overly ambitious youth he hands over the wings after defining their power in much more general terms than usual. Indeed the first property he claims for them is that of giving dominion over others (10/8) and the second is the widening of choice. Wearing them, you can choose among "a thousand things" (10/11–12). The wider implications of the opening scene are therefore not contradicted but embodied in a God whose prime weapon may be love, but not his only one. This is why the flight is described through analogies not only with Dido but also Icarus and Phaeton whose ignorance was coupled with youthful ambition rather than amorous longings.

This particular Cupid emerges fittingly from this particular landscape in another sense. Like the Nature which masks discordance and even viciousness under an appearance of beauty, he is a God of deceit. Always one of his characteristics, it is here given particular prominence. Most obviously it is enacted. From smiles and apparent beneficence he moves to cruel mockery and deserts the dreamer once he has nearly destroyed him. His appearance too, as a child willing to serve, conceals the reality of divine power. His darts are double and one of the major gifts he is willing to confer is the ability to 'beguile'. Even his speech relies on dual interpretations, so that when he dismisses the cost of his "geare" as "But rendring all againe", he knows the dreamer will interpret this as "just give me them back" but means "put yourself entirely in my power".

If Cupid is seen as the natural God to enter such a landscape because his temptation links love with desire more generally and because his duplicity and cruelty embody major features of that landscape, then of course it is misleading either to evaluate the poem as a solely erotic allegory or complain that a love poem suddenly turns into a moral one. The focus throughout is on man's total experience, in which love naturally looms large, especially in youth. That the dreamer is completely taken in need not be enlarged upon. From the moment he condescends to Cupid as "my child", he is lost, consistently and unquestioningly taking appearance for reality. Throughout, the wiser Narrator laments this ignorance and provides, in Stanza 14, a whole series of proverbs emphasising the need for experience and the importance of acting in accordance with the dictates of time.

But what is the dreamer in such a hurry to accept? Certainly it is not altruistic love. In fact he becomes Cupid's dupe so easily because he shares the cruel, lustful and ambitious aims offered by the God. Cupid offers "wanton wings"; the dreamer climbs with "wanton heart". Cupid tells him to shoot "somebody"; he fires "in hope to hurt another". There is no suggestion of romantic affection—anyone will do. The line "Desiring, impiring" sums up his position admirably. What he wants is dominion both in love and life. What he gets is the opposite—servility and frustrated desire. The Narrator, even at this early stage, anticipates characters in the psychomachia to follow when he attributes the fall to Wilfulness acting without the counterbalance of Skill or Reason.

Lurching from one extreme to another, the dreamer inevitably suffers an illness which involves an upsetting of the elements and humours. Fire and melancholy possess him, while his ignorance is symbolised by blindness. Montgomerie vividly presents a picture of the young lover withering away until he looks like a skeleton. But although it is specifically love which has caused him to suffer, it is the wider personification of Desire which is identified as the root cause and enters him the moment Cupido/Cupid disappears. That is, although the arrow specifically produced amorous desire, he is still ruled by the wider principle and so has not changed.

The other allegorical character aroused by the wound is Courage and our first impression of him is favourable. He sustains the dreamer when all seems lost and brings him to the vision of Hope and Despair without handing him over to the latter at once. The allegoric figures are beginning to assemble but also, for the first time, we see the Cherrie and the Slae. Later I shall discuss these in the context of possible symbolism. At this stage the dreamer is working only through the senses and I shall confine myself to noting their appearance and natural qualities for that is the level on which he is working and the Narrator makes no attempt to interpret for him.

In terms of his illness both fruits hold out the promise of liquid to ease the fire which possesses him and the dreamer, motivated by Desire, naturally prefers the sweetness of the Cherrie to the bitterness of the Slae. Although he presents himself as unable to make up his mind, the doubt does not set one fruit against the other. It concerns whether or not to attempt the difficult ascent which makes the Cherrie so difficult to reach. This is why a whole stanza is devoted to a—foreseeably—sensual description of that fruit, while the Slae is dismissed in one line:

> A bush of bitter slaes.
>
> (23/14)

It is also why his understanding of the difficulty focuses only on the ascent of the crag, ignoring the task of crossing the river, when later the council under Reason considers both. The spiritual implications of the river are not understood and only the most obvious practical problem concerns him in his ignorance. A further reason for discounting the Slae is that Courage is one of the first qualities to govern him. A difficult ascent naturally attracts that quality just as Desire naturally prefers the Cherrie's sweetness.

The fruits are therefore not initially introduced as equal contestants for the dreamer's attention, a situation which follows logically from his state as allegorically presented. Only one further factor is at this point relevant. Just as Montgomerie has chosen to use literary conventions in unexpected ways so he chooses to reverse at least one of the usual characteristics associated with his chosen fruits. It is the Slae whose difficulty of access is usually highlighted due to its prickly appearance. In this sense Jonson opposes its antecedent the wild plum to the pear in "To Penshurst" (lines 52–5).[14] The Cherrie, on the other hand, was associated with immediate gratification. It is not, therefore, the nature of the fruits themselves but their geographical setting, which determines the relative difficulty of the quests. And although the idea of two fruits being assessed in terms of their relative usefulness to man may suggest a 'conflictus' such as "The Violet and the Rose", both the unequal presentation of the combatants and the concentration on them as objects rather than active, speaking characters within the debate should prevent us from stressing the parallel too forcefully.

THE DEBATE IN IGNORANCE: DANGER'S DEFEAT AND VICTORY

That said, the remaining 87 stanzas (or over two-thirds of the poem) are essentially a series of debates, taking the dreamer from ignorance to understanding. In the last movement, when Reason draws the combatants towards harmony, the counter-arguments become more muted but even at that stage they do not disappear until the last moment. What must be decided is the precise nature of these debates and how, if at all, they fit into that broad tradition which has its origins in the Carolingian 'altercationes', Virgil's third contention eclogue, and Prudentius' *Psychomachia*.

The first extended allegorical contention covers Stanzas 27–44. From the dreamer's viewpoint it is accurate to call it the "Debate in Ignorance". As a separate character he says nothing, leaving what appears to be a negative trio—Danger, Dread and Despair—to pit their wits against Hope and Courage. Of these the first group seem to advocate the Slae and the second certainly press for the Cherrie. Now, many of these characters are familiar to us from the *Romance of the Rose*. But if we are thinking of this as a sort of re-run of the earlier poem (especially if we accept C. S. Lewis's view of it) a number of very real problems arise. Of these, the most striking is that the apparently positive voices of Hope and Courage are consistently mastered in argument and the wish of Danger that higher counsel should be sought is acted upon when Experience, Reason, Wit and Skill enter.

To understand this, four initial points must be grasped. *The Cherrie and the Slae* being a general rather than solely erotic allegory, the characters within it should not be interpreted only in amorous terms. Further, the allegory as it develops does not follow the pattern of *The Romance of the Rose* in having some characters neutral to the dreamer, some representing aspects of his personality and some representing the moods of the lady. In *The Cherrie and the Slae* all the characters depict the internal struggles of the dreamer. It is in that sense a strict 'battle for the soul'. Also, in assessing the degree to which the two sides press for Cherrie or Slae, one must not miss the very important distinction between the contingent and the absolute; between immediate and final goals. Last, although the sides are drawn up in the way I described, of the hesitant trio, at this stage only Danger speaks. Dread, like his equivalent in the *Romance*, maintains a lengthy silence, as much in keeping with his nature as is the nihilistic non-participation of Despair.

Once we understand the true significance of Danger, the apparent problems largely disappear. He is not a feature of the lady. He represents not her disdainfulness but a moral category applied to the dreamer and related to the etymological connection between Danger and 'dominium'—'power' or 'control'. It is significant that critics of the *Romance*, who view it in wider terms than Lewis, argue in a similar way and conclude that Danger stands for the power which the rational will exercises in specific instances.[15] That is why, in the *Romance*, he, like Fear and Shame, is "of the lineage of Lady Reason born". It is why, in *The Cherrie and the Slae*, he proves a better debater than emotional forces such as Hope and Courage. It is also why he longs to introduce more knowledgeable allies to the dreamer, for these will be able to translate into general principles his own, largely instinctive, reactions to each event as it comes.

Certainly any close analysis of the debate reveals him as more than a match for Hope and Courage. The latter's opening gambit in Stanza 27 consists of a self-contradiction (Don't listen to others/I have heard others say) and a false, one-sided view of Fortune as always supporting the strong. He follows this with a high-sounding call to aspire to great heights, the very course which the dreamer has just—disastrously—followed. Danger points out these similarities, reinforcing his argument with proverbs and authorities.He seizes on the idea of deceit, so relevant to Cupid, suggesting that his opponents embody it just as much as the God, and rightly argues that they are asking for another hurried ascent without learning lessons from the past. In addition they have defined the purpose of the quest wrongly and have failed to consider its future implications. Their thought, like Cupid's promises, covers "a thousand things" (cf. 10/12 and 32/5) but will serve to increase the dreamer's fire by once more defying the laws of Time.

His solution is a double one. First he suggests they turn to the Slae:

slake

> Yon Slae, suppose thou think it sowre
> Would satisfie to sloken
> Thy drouth now, of youth now,
> Which dries thee with desire;
> Assuage then, thy rage then,
> Foule water quencheth fire.

> (32/9–14)

This counsel is offered not as a final solution to spiritual problems, the level on which the dreamer's fate will finally be judged. It is intended as an immediate cure for a physical illness whose major symptoms are fire and melancholy. Interestingly, Culpeper in his seventeenth-century description of herbal remedies identifies the sloe-

bush as a plant of Saturn (melancholy) and a cure for
"fluxes" (excesses of the humours) while dismissing the
sweet variety of cherry as a tree of Venus (love) which,
though pleasant to taste, provides "little nourishment".[16]
Danger may, therefore, be the better physician. Certainly
this is the context of his hesitant, practical suggestion. A
long-term solution will also be necessary but, he argues,
none of the present debaters are qualified to give it. They
will need to call in

> . . . counsel yet ere ye conclude,
> Of wiser men then they.   (43/5–6)

This stage of the debate is rounded off in Stanza 44.
Danger suffers a physical defeat, for he retires. Allegorically this represents the mastery of weakness by strength,
earlier claimed by Courage. Intellectually he triumphs, for
the very council he had called for now appears. First, there
is Experience, indicating that the dreamer is beginning to
learn from the past. Secondly, there are the higher
qualities of the soul—Reason, Wit and Skill. But just as the
Debate in Ignorance is completed, so the next stage in the
dreamer's learning process begins. Experience addresses
not the dreamer but the quality which still wholly
dominates him and has been identified by the Narrator as
the true root of his problems—Will. And for Will there is
no doubt where the quest ends. He longs for the "lustie
Cherrie", his choice of adjective revealing the level of
judgement. The first words of the learned council are
intended to check his enthusiasm, although again it must
be noted that they criticise not the goal he has chosen but
his means of achieving it:

> Quoth they, "Is there no more adoe
> Ere yee win up the brae,
> But doe it, and to it,
> Perforce your fruit to pluck?
> Well brother, some other
> Were better to conduct."   (44/9–14)

The Debate in Confusion: the Overthrow of Will

Within the next section (Stanzas 45–76) Will becomes the central focus of yet another debate, being opposed by Experience, Reason, Skill and Wit.[17] The dreamer is in an intermediary stage of Confusion between Ignorance and Experience but does make progress, casting off the two extremes of Will and Despair. Finally he is able to speak in his own voice, giving a not unreasonable précis of what has happened to him so far. The overall plan, then, is clear and the heavy reliance on the debate tradition confirmed. The critic must ask a further question, however. Is the author not in danger of losing his reader's attention, having deprived himself of some of the more obviously dramatic techniques of the tradition? Argument prevails. The metaphor of the physical journey has been adopted but remains static until the internal debate is concluded. Dramatic metaphors such as that of battle are not emphasised. The symbols (so far vague and unequally represented) do not assume any greater importance, being elements in the argument but little more. That being so, does Montgomerie adequately turn argument into action or does his approach encourage vagueness and intellectualism to a degree which would justify the parodist of the eighteenth century who accused him (with specific reference to *The Cherrie and the Slae*):

> Of penning Poems at thy will
> And mask[ing] the matter with such skil
> As few perceave the drift?[18]

Even accepting the fact that a writer of that period might be out of touch with the conventions of Renaissance allegory, one must admit that these are the dangers the poet has chosen to run.

Certainly, one cannot deny the subtlety nor the complexity of the allegory. But the poet does keep changing the major contestants, while highlighting a different character in each section—in this instance moving from Danger to Will. In so doing he maintains dramatic variety and identifies the root cause of the dreamer's illness as defined by the Narrator ('13/11; 15/7). But Will, like Danger, Hope and Courage, is not seen as wholly evil. Like Lady Mede in *Piers Plowman* he may bring one or two out of every hundred to victory (53/1–8). A distinction is made between 'Will' (wilfulness), which is rejected, and 'will' as choice under reason, which is retained (67/3). Montgomerie, therefore, on the highest level is hoping to impress through the subtlety of his psychological argument but he does present the dispute in an interesting manner.

In other ways he aids his reader. First, he maintains a number of leitmotiv themes, answered differently by the characters at successive stages in the journey. In this section the most significant feature is the general agreement between members of the council and Danger. Will prefers single leadership to harmonious consultation. Reason and the others, in moving towards a solution in terms of a Platonic hierarchy of the Soul, merely take further the idea broached by Danger in Stanza 43. Will argues for extremes and indeed embodies one. Experience and the council in rejecting both Wilfulness and Despair put into operation the doctrine of the middle way stated by Danger in Stanza 32. The place of Time is also thoroughly discussed. Will, like Hope and Courage, believes that any time is a good time and equates success with speed. Experience and the council prefer the view, so often expressed in Montgomerie's lyrics, that one must act in accord with those laws of Time which show that action at the wrong moment may be catastrophic, or, as Skill puts it proverbially:

> 'The man that will not when he may,
>   He shal not when he would.'

(72/5–6)

This again confirms the view of Danger, voiced in Stanzas 29, 31, 37 and 49.

These thematic leitmotivs, drawing the reader like the dreamer slowly through the argument, are backed up by leitmotiv images, similarly employed. The most obvious are those concerned with the sea and fishing and that of the horse, again introduced by Danger in Stanza 29:

untimely   Untimous spurring spilles the stead.

                                                              (29/5)

The latter is particularly important because of its Platonic associations and will lead naturally into the Platonic hierarchy of the last movement. In the present debate Will is viewed as being only capable of mounting a Yuletide horse, while Reason makes the point more explicitly, when claiming that his "bridle wants a bit".

Montgomerie, then, is concerned primarily with argument as action. He tries to make that argument interesting through its subtlety and through varied characterisation. He regularly provides proverbial simplifications of major points. He gives his readers imagistic and thematic constants to guide them on the journey they share with the dreamer. But he also provides the variation of vivid drama. Reason's conventional argument that Will is worse than a beast does not remain a matter of scholastic dispute. Will *behaves* like a beast. He becomes "as angry as an ape"; runs "ramping, swearing rude and rape". The doctrine of the 'via media', central to the philosophy of James VI, is argued out but finally justified in the dramatic climax when Will goes mad and Despair hangs himself. This may be Montgomerie's most serious and most deeply philosophical poem but the author of 'The Navigatioun' and *The Flyting* is not one to forget the needs or limitations of his audience.

The two voices which round off this stage of the debate and lead into the next, have for different reasons been muted so far. The fact that they are now given lengthy speeches is a clear indication of the advances being made. The first speaker is the dreamer himself, viewed apart from the personified components of his character. He gives a reasonable précis of past events, stressing the distance he has come from the indecision of near despair to the "blest" alliance with Reason and his friends. At the equivalent stage of the earlier debate Will had answered on his behalf. This not only dramatises the fact that the death of Will gives the dreamer the freedom he has been craving, it also gives him a more rational nature. He talks in a calm, measured tone, much at odds with his earlier contributions which have lurched from ill-founded joy to despairing complaint. Reason and Experience are beginning to dominate his personality. They also give freedom to Dread, whose presence has been noted at an early stage but who has not yet uttered a word. The new situation, placing Hope and Courage, the major objects of his fear, in an impotent position, permits him to voice his views. Interestingly, he uses this opportunity to suggest that Will made the dreamer lean always towards the wishes of his opponents despite the superior arguments of Danger, an opinion which has been confirmed by the evidence of the poem.

THE DEBATE IN EXPERIENCE: THE DREAMER PROGRESSES

All this anticipates the "Debate in Experience" dominated by that character and consisting primarily of an uneven argument between him and 'Hope and Courage'. It is at this stage (stanzas 77–94) that the earlier Waldegrave text runs out and it is surely not improbable that the poet waited until later life to add the portion containing the lessons of his own experience.

The discussion is conducted throughout on a higher level and the advances presented in a variety of ways. The stress on Experience is the most obvious of these. But a clear distinction is also made between means and ends. Experience is primarily concerned with means and it is appropriate that he focuses on Hope and Courage, who have chosen the correct goal (the Cherrie), but are approaching it in the wrong way. He also lays stress on the new will of the dreamer—not wilfulness but choice. In choosing to listen to Experience and Reason, he is making their task easier because they cannot come "unrequyrde",

> But wee now, ye see now,
> Doe nothing undesirde.
>
> (77/13–14)

For the first time, too, religious concepts such as repentance and the doctrine of the Fall enter the poem, raising the level of allegorical emphasis and showing that the dreamer's definition of his goal changes as he becomes older. The latter doctrine, for example, is used to give a new twist to the Time leitmotiv. Ever since Adam and Eve, people have tried to take shortcuts to knowledge, encouraged by ignorant Hope.

These advances are made slowly and, as the earlier illustration suggests, by returning to earlier themes such as the laws of time, or the oppositions between reality and experience, extremes and moderation. Not only Hope and Courage but Dread and Danger continue to make some of their old errors. All four still see the problem in oversimplified terms; still claim victories over each other instead of working harmoniously and fail to see the all-important distinction between means and ends. Only in the last movement will everything become clear.

But this gradual progression, retaining many constants, makes it easier for the reader to note any advance that is made. Hope and Courage may still be unreconciled to the idea of the council and have to be convinced of Experience's status as a valid teacher but each is now moving under his sway and that of Reason. As a result, almost in spite of themselves, they begin to fall into line.

Hope can work in man's favour, as Experience points out in Stanza 82, although the odds are firmly against it:

> I would incace a count were crav'd.
> Shew thousand thousands thou
>   deceivde,
> Where thou was true to one.

$$(82/1-3)$$

The conditions for that single optimistic view are now being met and Hope's long speech, which immediately follows, confirms this. For the first time "weighing his words", he uses the leitmotiv image of the sea journey not (as in the past) to argue for more haste but to stress his value as an anchor in time of despair, and to identify the real villain as Ignorance. He is not fully aware of the positive implications of these remarks, a position which is cleverly conveyed by having him grow angry when Experience agrees, but he has for the first time stressed his true value and unconsciously argued for a process of learning rather than blind haste.

Courage also makes most of his old errors but again there is a major advance. In identifying love as the source of his support for the dreamer, he pinpoints a source of strength within his nature and sounds a more altruistic, less strident note than before. But he is still anxious for confrontation and, like Hope, fails to see that imperceptibly he is becoming an ally rather than an enemy of Experience. Dread and Danger, by way of contrast, are anxious to be corrected. When they err in presuming that every aspect of their counsel, including their earlier preference for the Slae, is going to be accepted, they are corrected, not by Experience whose lessons they know, but by Wit, the very character Danger had appealed to as early as Stanza 31. It is their acceptance of this subservience that Wit mentions and Experience expands upon. What may have seemed a valid temporal goal in

youth (the Slae) may not be a proper spiritual goal now.
Unlike their opponents they put up no opposition:

> They knew then, how true then,
> were not eager   And preasde not to reply.

(89/13–14)

This moment of transition, immediately prior to the
final movement from debate into harmony, from means to
ends, is an appropriate point to consider one of the trickiest
points of interpretation. *The Cherrie and the Slae* is the title of
the poem and the choice between them is about to be
made. We have accepted the obvious contrasts between
sweetness and sourness and noted the inversion of the usual
association of 'Cherrie' with ease of access and 'Slae' with
difficulty. In the early portion of the poem the emphasis on
erotic desire encouraged further connections with opposed
love objects, and the last discussion is going to set them in a
religious context. Can we go further and see them
foreshadowing either political problems such as the choice
between the crown of Scotland and that of England as well,
or make the religious opposition more specific and identify
the Cherrie with Catholicism and the Slae with Protestantism? This is a position held by Mrs Shire and one to which I
have earlier given guarded support.[19] It must still remain a
possible interpretation if only because Montgomerie's
refusal to assign definite labels to either of the fruits leaves
the reader a freedom of association within which such
oppositions could well have been intended.

All that later critics can validly do, however, is to study
the poem as closely as possible for signs and note the
opinion of commentators nearer in time to the work. Such
a study makes me even more hesitant than before. Analysis
of the work itself produces the following conclusions.
Neither the Cherrie nor the Slae is an obvious symbol for
the monarchy, Catholicism or Protestantism, so that
specific hints are necessary if these associations are to be
generally conveyed. But very few possible hints exist.

Indeed the Slae is descriptively dismissed in one line during the earliest debate; nor does it at any point provide the real opposition suggested by the dignity of the Scottish crown or the power of Protestantism. It is faintly advocated by Danger as an immediate physical cure in that part of the poem where it is briefly described. There it is set within a bush, the symbol of the Reformed church in France, but surely, even for a political allegory, the attention is too brief and conventional to alert even the inquiring mind? In terms of emphasis, the exact nature of the goals is subsidiary to a close examination of the means of approach—i.e., the psychology of the dreamer. The metaphors employed confirm that this is a universal allegory, able to accommodate particular aims, but striving to be a lesson for all men. In that universality lies the key to its popularity and on that universality critical stress must lie.

This still does not discount the possibility of a covert code known at court. The major reason for suspecting this comes from the poems of Duff. In the second, he refers to Montgomerie as an enemy of heresy and one who "attacked the 'Picards' both in arms and song". To infer from this a reference to *The Cherrie and the Slae* involves two hypotheses, each in itself quite likely but hypotheses nonetheless. First, the poem must have been set to music. As we have seen, the evidence for this is strong but not conclusive. Secondly, 'Picards' must mean Protestants. Duff does seem to equate these terms in another poem and he would not be the first writer to do so. Yet there was a rebellion in Picardy in which Montgomerie could have been involved, so that the surface meaning also remains possible. If Duff is saying that *The Cherrie and the Slae* is a fearless song written to support militant Catholicism, he is not himself saying it very fearlessly. Also, if he is the Latin translater of the poem, as Dilworth seems to have proved beyond reasonable doubt, he continues his evasiveness, describing it in his introduction as a work "De virtutum et

vitiorum pugna/Sive electio status in Adolescentia" (On
the battle of the virtues and/vices; or the choice of one's
condition in youth).[20] When he is so ambivalent and no
other early commentator known to me places the poem
within the framework of the Counter Reformation, it
seems to me that the presence of this line, even as a covert
message to a chosen few, must remain only an interesting
possibility.

RECONCILIATION UNDER REASON: THE CHERRIE GAINED

In brief descriptive terms, the last section of the poem
(stanzas 95–114) finds the Narrator turning to Reason,
who, after the last minor disagreements have been
silenced, maps out how the journey should be undertaken
and what the goal is to be. Establishing a harmonious
hierarchy in which both the council and the four
remaining disputants all have their place, he helps the
leader over the river and up the crag until he is ready to
seize the Cherrie. The fruit, however, obligingly falls from
the tree before they need to climb it. The Narrator
concludes by thanking God for his recovered health.

As usual, the transition between debate sections is
indicated by an appeal to the dreamer. Initially Will had
replied on his behalf; then he had spoken for himself,
intelligently weighing up past events. These moments had
accurately defined the stage of his spiritual journey and
anticipated the figure dominating the next section—first
Will and then Experience. The same technique is
employed in Stanza 95 and in answer to Experience's
challenge the dreamer does not just accept Reason, he
rushes to him:

> To Reason I was faine to flee,
> His counsell for to crave.   (95/5–6)

He is ready to learn the highest lessons and Reason "with
silver scepter in his hand" will assume the position of major
character in the drama.

But the final movement distinguishes itself from the earlier ones in two major ways. It maintains elements of the debate mode which has dominated the poem since Stanza 27 but by now the arguments are less intense. We return to the journey metaphor and the vision which the poet in youthful ignorance and near despair had viewed sensually and not understood. We return to this in experience, led by Reason. The differences are already marked and the true success of all the internal debates will only be confirmed if the journey is well managed and the correct fruit gained. But the debate, though muted, does not cease and one important feature stands out. For the first time it is Dread and Danger who become more troublesome. This is inevitable. The errors of Hope and Courage were made at the level of means—they always wanted action and the Cherrie. We are now concerned with ends and while Dread and Danger have not exactly advocated the Slae, instinctively they prefer it and are frightened by the prospect of an adventurous assault. Their fears do seem to be on the dreamer's behalf (104/3–6) and to stem from a clear awareness of their own limitations (104/1–14). That, however, is the full extent of their opposition. They agree that they gave up the right to final choice when first they asked for wiser council. Ironically at the last moment they need the support of their apparent enemies Hope and Courage to aid them. Hand in hand the four follow the leading party, a fitting emblem of reconciled opposites, unified by Reason.

This leads naturally into the second distinguishing feature. Reason's domination of the section differs from that of either Will or Experience because his task and his relationship to the dreamer differs. Will had dominated because he had controlled the personality of the dreamer. Experience had dominated because he was teaching the same figure. But Reason is the majestic controller of an overall plan in which he will delegate to others the functions for which they are most appropriate, reserving to himself the task of guiding the hierarchy, much as Reason controlled the horses of the appetites in Plato's *Republic*.

At the lower level we have seen him linking the four enemies in a new spirit of mutual aid. The tasks allotted to Skill and Wit are equally appropriate to their nature and their advice sheds new light on old themes. Skill, for example, has always been seen as practical knowledge. He is the doctor who can diagnose the cure for the dreamer's illness. Up until now he has refused to present his solution because Time has not been ripe:

> Far better late than never thrive
>
> (59/2)
>
> The man that will not when he may,
> He shal not when hee would.
>
> (72/5–6)

When he now speaks, identifying the Cherrie, we know that the optimum moment for action has arrived.

Wit primarily stands for theoretical knowledge, the learning which looks forward and interprets. As such he complements Experience, becomes the guide and chooses the route. By discussing first two extreme plans and then preferring the one which is neither over-rash nor over-cautious, he confirms the doctrine of moderation. They will skirt the waterfall, crossing at a shallow place, giving a reasonable route up the crag. As he describes, he also interprets the vision spiritually. The depth of the stream represents the "running dead" and the quest is therefore an otherworldly one, the Cherrie now a religious symbol.

Here, iconographical and literary traditions are helpful. In Christian iconography the cherry symbolises the sweetness of character deriving from good works and is sometimes held to be the Fruit of Paradise.[21] Its white and red fruit had also suggested flesh and blood and therefore the Eucharist. The dreamer in the centre of his company of reconciled qualities therefore comes to be judged at the highest court. In this context the emphasis on the source of the river flowing from a "pretty spring" and the falling of the fruit of its own accord strongly suggests acceptance through grace, the divine gift which even the most righteous must receive before entering into salvation. Grace is often presented as stemming from a small spring and is, according to Aquinas, ready for the prepared Christian at all times. The fact that one receives it as a gift and does not seize it as fitting reward is movingly conveyed in the apparent anti-climax[22] of the physical journey which marks the real climax of the spiritual quest.

The dreamer's journey through life has taken him from the lowest levels of earthly love and the despair they caused to the highest levels of divine charity and a joy which will last forever. The all-important final stanza, which is no conventional rounding-off topos, but a heartfelt cry of gratitude, defines the latter state with Montgomerie's usual eloquence:

> Praise be to God, my Lord, therefore,
> Who did mine health to mee restore,
> Being so long time pinde.
> Yea, blessed bee his holy Name,
> Who did from death to life recleame
> Mee, who was so unkinde.
> All nations also magnifie
> This everliving Lord.
> Let me with you and you with mee,
> To laude him ay accord.
> Whose love ay we prove ay
> To us above all things;
> And kisse him and blesse him,
> Whose glore eternall rings.

(114/1–14)

The frequent use of 'me', 'my' and 'mine' reminds us that although this is a 'maniefalde allegorie' moving from worldly blindness to divine enlightenment and teaching lessons to everyone ("all nations"), these lessons are based on personal experience. Although this final stanza proclaims the ultimate optimism of the believer, the joy of final union with God has been set against a background which highlights the difficulties of attaining it. Only if you win the inner moral battle, ruthlessly rejecting extreme evils such as Wilfulness and Despair, while bringing potentially destructive and naturally opposed qualities into a state of harmonious co-existence under the guidance of Experience and the control of Reason will this reward be given. Even then God in his grace must will it and the many false opportunities proffered by Time be scorned. It would have been strange had Montgomerie, a man beset by so many difficulties in his own life, produced a vision of life's pilgrimage which underestimated the difficulties involved. As it is, he accentuates the value of the "cherrie" by making its possession the outcome of such a long and dangerous struggle.

   The Cherrie and the Slae is not only Montgomerie's major poem, it is also his finest achievement. As usual, adopting a stanza which will show off his verbal dexterity and formal control to best effect, he has drawn creatively from past traditions to produce one of the subtlest Renaissance allegories known to me. Scorning obviously dramatic metaphors such as that of battle and following Langland in adopting the metaphor of physical quest only to stop progress in the name of intellectual debate, he has relied (until the very last moment) on his ability to make the inner disagreements and conflicting aims of the personality so interesting in and for themselves, that the reader's attention is held throughout. The movement from initial vision through debates of Ignorance, Confusion and Experience to final harmony and solution gives a clear pattern to follow. Leitmotivs of theme and image, which are reinterpreted as the dreamer learns and the allegorical emphasis changes, give further aid, as do the proverbial simplifications of complex truths. And if we are expected to follow lengthy debates on profound topics and note slight but crucial changes of attitude or interpretation, the pace is gradual; contrasting characters dominate the successive arguments and moments of crisis are often presented in a vividly dramatic manner. In these ways Montgomerie seeks to make his poem accessible to all without compromising the desire to present a complex view of life. The poem's continued popularity suggests that he succeeded, even if, in Boccaccio's terms, not every reader could be expected to pierce each of the allegory's many 'veils'.

NOTES

1. John Pinkerton, *Ancient Scottish Poems*, London, 1786, p. cxviii.
2. C. S. Lewis, *The Allegory of Love*, Oxford, 1936, p. 259.
3. Shire, *Song, Dance and Poetry, op. cit.*, pp. 171–2.
4. *Montgomery MSS, op. cit.*, p. 400.
5. Lewis, *op. cit.*, p. 259.
6. *Historia Ecclesiastica Gentis Scotorum*, Bannatyne Club, II, 496.
7. Cranstoun, *op. cit.*, p. xxix.
8. Ian Ross, "The Form and Matter of *The Cherrie and the Slae*", *Texas Studies in English*, XXXVII, 1958, pp. 79–91.
9. Shire, *op. cit.*, pp. 117–38.
10. Ross, *op. cit.*, p. 91.
11. Shire, *op. cit.*, pp. 130–7.
12. The visions must be part of a dream, although the Narrator (1/14) only wonders if he is asleep.
13. Henryson's 'Preiching of the Swallow', for example, contains a similar hunter and is referred to directly in Stanza 14.
14. I am grateful to Professor A. D. S. Fowler for pointing this out.
15. John V. Fleming, *The Roman de la Rose: A Study in Allegory and Iconography*, Princeton, 1969, pp. 188–9.
16. This book did not appear until 1653. It does not prove Danger's diagnosis to be the correct one, but gives evidence of a belief that may have been earlier held.
17. I have taken the view that Wit and Wisdom are the same character. Wit is introduced accompanying Reason at Stanza 44 but it is Wisdom who speaks in Stanzas 51, 53 and 56. From Stanza 59 until the end only Wit is identified.
18. *A Facetious Poem in Imitation of The Cherry and the Slae*, Edinburgh, 1701, Stanza 4.
19. *A Choice of Scottish Verse 1560–1660*, ed. R. D. S. Jack, London, 1978, p. 20.

20. *Cerasum et Sylvestre Prunum*, Arctaunum, 1631; Mark Dilworth, "The Latin Translator of *The Cherrie and the Slae*", *Studies in Scottish Literature*, V, 1967, pp. 77–82.
21. George Ferguson, *Signs and Symbols in Christian Art*, New York, 1961, p. 29.
22. In the sense that the Cherrie falls from the tree which "could not be clum" (climbed).

CHAPTER VI

WHERE NOW?

In answering the question posed by the title of this chapter, I must return to the issues raised briefly in the Preface. For a long time in Scottish Literary studies no other writers were allowed to emerge from the gigantic shadows cast by Burns and Scott. Fortunately we have now advanced a good distance from that situation. But some authors still lurk in undeserved obscurity. Montgomerie is one of these and I make no secret of the fact that my major aim in writing this book has been to rescue him from a new shadow—that cast in Mediaeval and Renaissance studies by the earlier makars Henryson, Dunbar and Douglas.

His claims to this recognition seem to me as many and varied as his undoubted rhetorical talents. *The Cherrie and the Slae* which, I have argued, is a more subtle and profound allegory than has generally been appreciated, may well still be his major achievement but his dramatic skills, the vigorous invective of *The Flyting* and the very different literary abilities shown in his lyrics and sonnets surely warrant extended analysis. Both as the accepted leader of James's 'Scottish Renaissance' and as a gifted poet in his own right he deserves much wider scholarly attention than that revealed by the Bibliography at the end of this book.

That Bibliography includes only works primarily concerned with the poet. He has, of course, also been assessed in Histories of Scottish Literature or in extended treatments of specific kinds of verse such as C. S. Lewis's *The Allegory of Love*. But, for the most part, these studies tend to support the older vision of him as the last (and least) of the makars, judging him according to criteria defined by the achievement of earlier authors. I do not wish to suggest that he is a finer poet than Henryson or Dunbar, for he is not; only that he should be judged on his own terms. Inevitably the approaches outlined above minimise an originality which the author is not concerned to find and underestimate a range of experiment which he has not the space to examine.

Those works listed in the Bibliography and their chronological span leave me in no doubt as to where the first advance must come. The very first entry for 1887 is also the last attempt at a full edition of his works. Cranstoun's editorial work is by no means poor. He is a reasonably careful editor if a superficial and derivative critic. But, as I have argued, there are inaccuracies and he did not have access to all the texts now available. For the lyrical verse we need a new edition of the Ker MS in particular, correcting misreadings, while preserving the original order, numbering and titles. *The Flyting* too must be re-edited and this promises to be a task of some magnitude, given the variety of versions available. I have followed the lead of most recent critics in using the Tullibardine MS as copy and have filled the gap it leaves at the beginning with the first Hart edition of 1621, a text to which Cranstoun did not have access. While this procedure may serve for the purposes of providing quotations in a work of criticism, my researches have shown that the editorial problems are more extensive than this somewhat simplistic solution suggests. The Tullibardine MS, although it is probably the oldest extant text and certainly the one which preserves the largest number of Scots words, also uses many forms nowhere else employed by Montgomerie. Of these, some suggest mishearing so that it may well be, at least in part, a memorially contaminated report. I make no pretence of having examined this problem in detail but it does not seem to me that any one text stands out as being demonstrably superior to the others.

Critical work has not only been sparse; it has come in short bursts separated by fairly long silences. At the turn of the century the two German theses by Hoffmann and Brotanek concentrated mainly on biography, sources and stylistic features. They are both quite thorough, if rather pedestrian, contributions. Nonetheless, until the present volume they were the only short books devoted entirely to Montgomerie. The most important critical advance was made in the mid and late sixties. It was led by Mrs Shire whose work on the musical dimension to his work is, for the most part, excellent. In *Song, Dance and Poetry of the Court of Scotland under King James VI* she was also the first to unite the earlier biographical researches of Stevenson with those of later scholars, notably Mark Dilworth. The seventies, however, passed the poet by in almost complete silence and it is only to be hoped that the return of interest in the early eighties may, for the first time, be sustained.

My own belief is that, to date, most of the literary criticism (including my own latest article) has been too biographically oriented. This is quite understandable as it has accompanied major new discoveries about Montgomerie's life while the poet's own writing often deals directly or indirectly with his personal problems. It can, however, lead us into dangerous areas, working from the life back to the literature instead of giving the latter prime attention. I would, therefore, hope that future work might follow the example of Ian Ross whose study of *The Cherrie and the Slae* combined sensitive analysis with an admirable understanding of the traditions which influenced the poet.

Above all, I trust that critics now and in the future will "wisely weigh" the words of James VI, when he urged the Castalians to

> Remember on Montgomeries flowand
>   grace,
> His suggred stile, his weightie words
>   divine

> And how he made the sacred Sisters
>   nine
> There montaine quitte to follow on his
>   trace.[1]

His 'maister poete' deserves no less.

NOTES

1. *Poems of James, op. cit.*, I, 108.

SELECT BIBLIOGRAPHY

1885–1910

   Editions
   The Poems of Alexander Montgomerie, ed. James Cranstoun, STS, 1887.
   The Poems of Alexander Montgomerie (Supplementary Volume), ed. George Stevenson, STS, 1910.

   Criticism
   O. Hoffman, *Studien zu Montgomerie*, Altenburg, 1894.
   R. Brotanek, *Untersuchungen über das Leben und die Dichtungen Alexander Montgomeries*, Vienna, 1896.

1911–1950

   Editions
   The Cherrie and the Slae, ed. H. Harvey Wood, London, 1937.

   Criticism
   Lois Borland, "Montgomerie and the French Poets of the Early Sixteenth Century", *Modern Philology*, XI, 1913–14.
   C. M. Maclean, *Alexander Scott, Montgomerie and Drummond of Hawthornden as lyric poets*, Cambridge, 1915.

1951–1970

   Editions
   Alexander Montgomerie: A Selection from his Songs and Poems, ed. Helena M. Shire, Saltire Society, 1960.

   Criticism
   K. Elliott, *Music of Scotland 1500–1700*, 2 vols., Cambridge dissertation, 1954 (Volume I unpublished; Volume II published as Elliott and Shire, *Music of Scotland 1500–1700*, Musica Britannica, XV, 2nd Edition, London, 1964).
   Ian Ross, "The Form and Matter of *The Cherrie and the Slae*", *Texas Studies in English*, XXXVII, 1958.
   Mark Dilworth, "New Light on Alexander Montgomerie", *The Bibliotheck*, IV, 1965.
   H. M. Shire, "Alexander Montgomerie. The oppositione of the court to conscience . . ." *Studies in Scottish Literature*, III, 1966.
   R. D. S. Jack, "Montgomerie and the pirates", ibid.

Mark Dilworth, "The Latin Translator of *The Cherrie and the Slae*", *Studies in Scottish Literature*, V, 1967.

H. M. Shire, *Song, Dance and Poetry of the Court of Scotland under King James VI*, Cambridge, 1969.

R. D. S. Jack, "The Lyrics of Alexander Montgomerie", *Review of English Studies*, XX, 1969.

1971–1984

Editions

A Choice of Scottish Verse 1560–1660, ed. R. D. S. Jack, London, 1978.

Criticism

Priscilla Bawcutt, "The Art of Flyting", *Scottish Literary Journal*, X, 1983.

R. D. S. Jack, "The Theme of Fortune in the Verse of Alexander Montgomerie", ibid.

John Durkan, "The Date of Alexander Montgomerie's Death", *Innes Review*, XXXIV, 1983.